THE MARXIST SYSTEM

CHATHAM HOUSE STUDIES IN POLITICAL THINKING

SERIES EDITOR: George J. Graham, Jr.
Vanderbilt University

THE
MARXIST SYSTEM

*Economic, Political, and
Social Perspectives*

ROBERT FREEDMAN
Colgate University

CHATHAM HOUSE PUBLISHERS, INC.
Chatham, New Jersey

THE MARXIST SYSTEM
Economic, Political, and Social Perspectives

CHATHAM HOUSE PUBLISHERS, INC.
Post Office Box One
Chatham, New Jersey 07928

PUBLISHER: Edward Artinian
COVER DESIGN: Antler & Baldwin Design Group Inc.
PRODUCTION SUPERVISOR: Chris Kelaher
COMPOSITION: Chatham Composer
PRINTING AND BINDING: Banta Company

LIBRARY OF CONGRESS CATALOGING-IN-PUBLICATION DATA

Freedman, Robert, 1921-
    The Marxist system : economic, political, and social perspectives
/ Robert Freedman.
        p. cm. -- (Chatham House studies in political thinking.)
    Bibliography: p.
    Includes index.
    ISBN 0-934540-31-4
    1. Marx, Karl, 1818-1883.   I. Title.   II. Series.
HX39.5.F67   1989
335.4'092'4--dc 19   86-23275
                                                              CIP

Manufactured in the United States of America
10   9   8   7   6   5   4   3   2   1

CONTENTS

Contents

ACKNOWLEDGMENTS

I wish to express my thanks to the following persons for helping to make this manuscript readable and as error free as is humanly possible: my thanks to Ilse Salomon, Jan Zieger, and Mary Dirlam Freedman who read the entire manuscript and helped to keep the prose within the bounds of the English language. Special thanks are due my typists, Lois Wilcox, Carol Alton, and Pat Ryan.

PREFACE

The influence of Karl Marx and Frederick Engels on the contemporary world is unquestionable. Engels, Marx's lifelong friend and collaborator, credited Marx with a fundamental intellectual breakthrough in the understanding of human history, the way institutions are formed by class conflict under capitalism, and what the human race eventually could hope to realize.

At Marx's graveside, Engels said that his friend had made two discoveries of unsurpassed importance. These were "the law of development of human history [and] the special law of motion governing present-day capitalist mode of production and the bourgeois society that this mode of production has created."

The first, the materialist conception of history, holds the sensible view that people must satisfy their basic needs for food, shelter, and clothing before they can pursue matters of the mind and spirit. Indeed, the level of economic development "form[s] the foundation upon which state institutions, the legal system, art, and even ideas on religion" are based.[1]

The second discovery was a demonstration of how, within present society, the exploitation of the worker by the capitalist takes place. The materialist interpretation of history, which places heavy emphasis on the primacy of economics, has often been looked upon as a denigration of the human race. Marx has been said to believe that humans are motivated solely by the desire for monetary gain and comforts and have no genuine ethical, moral, or spiritual needs. Indeed, the entire thrust of Marx's criticism of capitalism is based on the perceived violations of minimal morality upon which capitalism rests.

On the contrary, Marx thought highly of the human race. He was certain that with the realization of communism—which over a long period of time would come to replace capitalism—humans could be released from their environment and thereby freed to develop their spiritual selves. Marx the historical materialist stood for the ideal of human emancipation in a world of peace and plenty. He believed in the prospect that human beings would one day live in a world that would enable them to achieve their full potential.

But the material world of nature had to be mastered and basic human physical needs satisfied before this potential could be realized. And to attain this goal, society had to organize to produce. Marx held that each level of economic development required a distinct form of economic organization. The advent of machinery that could vastly increase productive work provided the most advanced form of economic organization, capitalism. But capitalism had social and economic consequences. As an economic system, it required, as did every system of production, the division of labor. In capitalism the goad of hunger forced people who did not own the means of production to sell their labor power; workers were thereby alienated from their true selves.

Capitalism enhanced the power of the bourgeoisie, the class that possessed the means of production, over the proletariat, the class that had to sell its labor power to meet physical needs. Capitalists owned tools while laborers possessed only their own labor power. Laborers, to live, were forced to sell their services to tool owners on unfavorable terms. The inequality in power between those who owned the means of production and those who did not marked the distinction between the bourgeoisie and the proletariat.

Inequality of economic condition meant inequality of political and social condition. Values and beliefs in society justified unequal economic relations; the bourgeoisie dominated by right every aspect of social life. What was probably most important about this fact for Marx was that exploitative relationships degraded and dehumanized people, making them selfish and cruel. One's fundamental capacity to be productive and to perceive oneself as a creative being was corrupted by the division of people into owners of the tools of creation and those who must sell their creative capacity.

Yet Marx eulogized capitalism. He argued that capitalism was the only system that could produce the tools of production necessary to set humankind free. Only this system, feeding on the greed of the capitalist, could provide the resources necessary to meet human needs so that an economy of abundance could arise. Only with the potential of the productive means developed by capitalism could men and women become fully human. The ever-increasing suffering of the proletariat under capitalism had a purpose. Suffering served as the precondition of ultimate freedom. The capitalist means of production are essential to the arrival of socialism. Suffering prepares the stage for revolution.

The bourgeoisie mistook their temporary and transient role in the great plan of history for an ideal and everlasting social order. They accepted as natural the class system and its supporting institutions. They looked upon the existing organization of state, law, religion, and family as divinely inspired. Marx held that these institutional forms merely reflected the underlying economic system and tried to show that they were ephemeral. Capitalism was the last and most important phase in the continuous evolution of history toward communism.

In Marx's view the bourgeoisie, like all previous owner classes, developed ideologies to support and justify class position. The bourgeoisie, supported by such ideology, used the power of the state to resist change. Eventually the proletariat, spurred by their own suffering and tutored by revolutionary intellectuals, would correctly see the world as it really was and seize power. They would usher in the ideal social order and eventually achieve the goals toward which all history pointed.

While Marx believed that the eventual revolt of the proletariat was a step built into history, he also believed that theoretical understanding of history should be used to guide action. Marx believed that it was possible to know the real world only by acting upon it and that, by acting, one changed it. Once one understood history, one should act upon that theoretical grasp.

Marx's theory of history was evolutionary and optimistic. He did not subscribe to a conspiracy theory. His system required no scapegoats. Capitalist and laborer alike were locked together in a symbiotic relationship, playing out their respective roles in creating ever-increasing wealth at the cost of ever-increasing misery for the working class. Ultimately, out of the contradictory dialectical conflict in which the capitalist and proletariat performed their roles, there was to arise a new organization of production—a society that was without classes because it was no longer based on exploitation. All would create, not because they were forced to it by the human condition, but because they were motivated to contribute to the human family.

Engels's claim that Marx had discovered "the laws of human history" meant that Marx's socialism was "scientific" in contrast to the "utopian" socialism of such predecessors and contemporaries of his as Owen, Saint-Simon, Proudhon, Weitling, and others. Engels wrote that all these men saw socialism as "the expression of absolute truth, reason, and justice, [which] has only to be discovered to conquer all the world by virtue of its own power." Marx's scientific socialism, which sought to discover the causes and cures of social misery and strife, required an analysis of the events of economic history.

Marxism was scientific, wrote Engels, because it tried to utilize a model of capitalist development derived from a study of the "real" world. Marx believed that "utopians" could only cry out against the world, not change it. Utopians believed that they could mentally construct ideal social systems and that men of reason and goodwill would, enlightened by persuasive argument, effectuate them. Marx endeavored to organize the latent power of the working class for political action.

Marx taught that self-directed "interests" compelled human actions. While the utopians looked inward to their own thought for solutions to social problems, Marx studied society. Marx's discovery of the objective laws of social change elevated the study of society from useless speculation to science. Marx held in high contempt what he considered the fruitless daydreams of do-gooders and romantic revolutionaries. He condemned the economists J.B. Say and Thomas Malthus—the first for his groundless optimism about the economy's capacity to regulate itself, the second for his libel of the human race in maintaining that it could destroy itself through overpopulation.

In this book I am concerned with two aspects of the story of Marxism. First is the Marxist System as a whole: How do its parts relate to one another? Second is the Marxist System in historical perspective: The book asks some fundamental questions about Marxism, after the more than 140 years of its existence as an intellectual system and as a guide.

Marx was one of the last of the great speculative philosophers to attempt to show the connection of all things in the universe to one another. He was a Renaissance man who took all knowledge as his province, who sought to understand and interpret the flow, purposes, and direction of history. He was a child of the Enlightenment in that he believed that human destiny lay in the hands of people rather than being determined by a benevolent deity.

Faith in the promise of science had grown enormously since the sixteenth century, when Francis Bacon and his successors suggested the possibility that the secrets of the universe were extractable by scientific investigation. Marx believed that scientific principles also governed human affairs. To Marx it seemed wholly plausible that once the secrets of nature were clearly seen, as they would be when historical conditions were right, all problems would be solved.

Marx was a descendant of the German romantic and historical philosophic tradition as well as a child of the Western Enlightenment. He saw the ultimate triumph of humankind not as a victory of the principle of rationality, but a consequence of an inevitable historical process.

Did Marx attempt to explain too much? The verdict of most people has been that Marx was too ambitious. His intellectual roots in the philosophy of the Enlightenment and German historicism by way of Hegel led him to expect too much of his fellow humans. Have his overly optimistic expectations been partly responsible for the disasters of the twentieth century—and do they signal the demise of Marxism both as a theory and a program? This question is addressed in chapter 12.

I discuss the Marxist System mostly in Marx's language. Some of the text is quoted nearly verbatim. The citations are from the original texts. The speculative discussion of the future of Marxism is, of course, my own.

CHAPTER 1

INTRODUCTION

More than 140 years ago, Europe was aflame with revolt. The year 1848 saw uprisings, sporadic and generally ineffectual, in Austria, Germany, Hungary, Italy, and elsewhere, but not in England.

That year was also the date of the publication of *The Communist Manifesto* by Karl Marx and Frederick Engels. The *Manifesto,* one of the most influential political documents ever written, declared war upon the emergent bourgeoisie in the name of the industrial proletariat.

Marx believed that the revolutions in Europe were the second phase of the revolt of humankind against economic exploitation and tyranny. The first had been the American and French revolutions of 1775 and 1789, both led by the bourgeoisie and undertaken to establish the political and economic ascendancy of capitalism. The "Rights of Man" proclaimed by these uprisings seemed to Marx to be in truth the rights of property. But in 1848, so Marxist analysis ran, the proletariat was in revolt against the consequences of the industrial revolution, against the slavery of capitalism.

Contrary to Marx's views, only in England, and to a lesser extent in France, was there a significant industrial proletariat. Yet there was no revolt in England, and where it broke out on the Continent, it was antiauthoritarian, antimonarchical, and antifeudal, largely middle class in origin. In England the landed aristocracy gave way or merged with the bourgeoisie. Political and economic reform kept revolution at bay.

Between the middle of the nineteenth century and World War I, Marxism and dozens of more or less coherent reformist and radical protest movements rose in response to the social upheaval brought by the industrial revolution. Marx's argument was that the central institutions of capitalism, which were private property, market-determined prices of nonhuman resources, and wage labor, threatened existing social arrangements, the power and wealth of landed aristocracy and the subservience and mere subsistence of peasants. Increasing misery was, he declared, the general condition in Europe. In fact, however, the living standard in England and much of Europe was slowly rising.

Much else was afoot during the period of the "great transformation," the turbulent hundred years between Waterloo and World War I. Farflung empires arose. Britain, France, Russia, and the United States dominated and annexed vast parts of the world. Older conflicts emerged within nation states. Ancient concerns, which had been temporarily submerged in larger political units, resurfaced. The descendants of ancient tribal peoples reaffirmed allegiances to land and ethnicity and to their near relatives, language, and religion.

Marx ignored these older and intractable motivations, arguing that capitalism and the class system that it spawned had far greater relevance to the human condition and to behavior. Economics superseded all else.

With faith characteristic of the Enlightenment, Marx confidently accepted the enormous challenge of trying to understand the place of humans in the cosmos. He made it his task to interpret the world in terms of social processes. He would transform modes of thought from speculation to science, from acceptance of the consequences of fate to purposeful human activity. Marx, as a true child of his time, firmly believed that the prospects for human achievement through science were limitless. He ignored such darker implications as the use of science for the destruction of human beings and even of the planet itself.

Marxism as a concept and a creed has flourished for nearly 150 years, during which its death has been continuously announced. Yet, like Antaeus, the giant wrestler of Greek mythology, Marxism has appeared until now to spring up mightier each time it was cast to the ground. Up to now no Hercules has succeeded in strangling Marxism in midair.

This chapter looks at some of the reasons for Marxism's long-lived appeal and discloses the plan of the book.

The Appeal of Marxism

Marxism connects everything that happens on the face of the planet with Marx's view that economic factors determine the course of history. Marx assumes that all social institutions can be understood from the premises of economic analysis and its handmaiden, class analysis. Armed with that understanding, society can reorder itself to suit its purposes.

The state is the tool of the ruling economic class. It protects private property and keeps social peace. This means that all gains by workers merely represent strategic retreats by rulers concerned to protect their own long-term interests. Schools and churches are instruments of education and comfort. The former function to inculcate reverence for the society as it is and at the same time to train the workforce; the latter give comfort to the hopeless, the losers who are consolingly assured that losing is only in this life.

It follows from this analysis that love of country is no more than love of one's oppressor. Nationalism is a hoax in the service of capitalism. People must therefore reconsider their loyalties. Workers, exploited in every country, must unite with one another against common oppressors.

Theory must be joined with practice. What is theory good for if it is not a guide to action? Marx's central ideas, historical materialism and the theory that labor alone creates value, derive from the philosopher Georg Wilhelm Friedrich Hegel (see chapters 2 and 6) and the English economist David Ricardo (see chapters 9 and 10). These two major concepts, converted by Marx for his own purposes, provide the theoretical underpinning for the conclusion that people have been duped and raped for private profit. And, predictably, this critical view of capitalism had resonance for depressed peoples everywhere. Socialism, which according to Marx was to emerge from the class struggle in the twilight of capitalism, has most often arisen in Third World settings that were more feudal than capitalist.

Prophetic Marxism foresaw that the contradictions inherent in capitalism would cause it to annihilate itself. Instead, capitalism has flourished. The societies that in Marx's time were capitalist political democracies have survived as such. The appeal of Marxism has not been to the industrial proletariat in the developed world but to disappointed intellectuals, politicians, and inhabitants of woefully poor, underdeveloped countries. Often educated in the West, some in Marxist-dominated universities, members of the elite found a reason for their country's backwardness in capitalist exploitation. For them Marxism provided both an explanation and a program. A direct route to socialism, so they thought, would avoid the misery of a capitalist-dominated industrial revolution.

Modern Marxists in the West, particularly sociologists and anthropologists, believe they can explain much of human history by use of Marxist analysis. A smaller group of economists find Marxist explanations compelling. But Western intellectuals who are Marxists have separated theory and practice. It is no longer widely held that a theory necessarily implies a policy.

Marxist and non-Marxist critics of contemporary Western society need not look far for examples of the low quality of so many lives even in rich countries. For the former, Marxism provides an answer. Inequality of condition is often unmitigated by equality of opportunity. Social and cultural differences, often accompanied by ethnic and color prejudices, seem to frustrate even non-Marxists with good intentions. In a market society, almost all who would prosper must succeed in the market. Many, by temperament or through lack of skills, find themselves excluded from the rewards of a market society.

Marxist and non-Marxist critics of capitalist civilization have different views of the causes of the misery of the underclass. Marxists stigmatize all those who accept inequalities in income, power, and status characteristic of capitalist societies, as apologists for the inhumanities of capitalism. They view reformers who would ameliorate the suffering of the working class by means of social programs as not understanding that, under capitalism, power is structural and intransigent; misery is inherent. For ameliorists, the civilizing influence of art, music, and literature can be a source of immediate enrichment for all. To the Marxist, the masses need real economic power before they can be in a position to enjoy better things.

For the ameliorist, education can inculcate proper values and curb the inordinate hunger of the bourgeoisie for money and status. For the Marxist, the system itself creates greed and corruption. Marxism appeals because it is the bearer of good tidings. Hegel's philosophy points not simply to a brighter but to an ideal future. And it is a secular theory promising salvation not in heaven but in the world. Suffering is not in vain; freedom and a release from pain will surely come when and where they are needed—here on earth, now. The bourgeois state emancipates serfs by law only to place them in thralldom to their capitalist masters. Marxism promises true freedom in a classless society.

True to Enlightenment doctrine, Marx believes that people have their destinies in their own hands. They need not accept misery as an inevitable component of life. Human beings can change things; history is on their side. Marx said what millions of people want to hear. His appeal, then, was one of hope.

The Marxist mode of thought has explanatory power. What is social science for, if not to analyze, interpret, explain, and predict? For many, Marxism seems able to explain war, poverty, unequal education, racism, colonialism, and the bankruptcy of culture. A great attraction of Marxism is the ease with which world events can be fitted into its system of assumptions. The theory of classes that explains that owners (the bourgeoisie) have a strong self-interest in perpetuating their wealth and power against the proletariat goes a great distance in explaining the behavior of governments.

There is verisimilitude in Marxism. It provides an insight into events that goes beyond the platitudes usually provided as explanations by apologists for capitalism. Look again at education. The Marxist urges: It is heavily supported by the public and by corporations. Yet it is widely held that education enhances democracy and provides equality of opportunity for the least privileged. But thoughtful people, the Marxist suggests, may not view education as a touching example of our society's generosity to the younger generation. They may ask whether the quality of education is not closely related to the social class of the students. They may perceive that the children of the bourgeoisie benefit

4

most and that children of the poor get just enough education to provide a supply of semiskilled and docile workers. This widely observed phenomenon is a central component of Marxist social analysis.

Today, however, the central appeal of Marxism seems to be on the wane. The appeal for a program of action, implied rather than stated by Marx, has lost many adherents, while Marxist programs embodied in the governmental policies of the Soviet Union, Eastern Europe, and Third World countries face disintegration. On the other hand, Marxism still seems able to explain existing policy in capitalist countries. Or does it? Can Marxism the theory survive its death as practice? Such considerations are addressed in chapter 12.

The Scope of Marxist Thought

Marxism is a philosophy, that is, a system of principles, of laws that regulate the universe. It is a theory of social change, a teleology that tells where history is heading. Within this framework, Marx's social science can be understood. He views the vastness of history and concludes that all of history is the "history of class struggles," by which he means the process by which change occurs. Its mechanism is class struggle.

Dialectical materialism is the form that the struggle takes. First, there is the existing world, the world as it is. This is the *thesis*. Within that world is contained the seeds of its own destruction, the *antithesis*. Thesis and antithesis cannot endure much tension. As the two forces struggle for the same turf, an explosion results. Both are destroyed, yet both are reborn in new and "higher" forms—for a Hegelian like Marx, a better form. The new form, in turn, has its own contradiction or tensions within itself. Again an explosion occurs, and a new and higher form of civilization develops.[1]

When Marx shifts from philosophy to economics, he broadens the scope of his inquiry and spawns a variety of theories. One inquiry concerns the theory of classes, previously mentioned; beyond that he posits theories of religion, alienation, state and law, marriage and family life, ideology, and civil liberties and freedom. All ideologies and institutions are seen as aspects of a superstructure that must be (or become) in harmony with the underlying reality of the relationship between the predominant economic classes, which in turn must be consistent with the existing mode of production. "Mode of production" means more than the technological means (or forces) involved in production. It refers to the way the economy is conducted: the private-property system (in our time) and the market and contractual relationships embodied in law. The mode of production in any society defines for that society its economic and social relationships.

For Marx, economics is always central. The way people organize the production and distribution of goods and services is the most important element of social life, although by no means the only one. All institutions are important. But first among more or less equals is the economy. How human beings produce, exchange, and allocate scarce resources among themselves is the key to how well society functions.

From that common-sense position, Marx moves outward. The nature of capitalism is such that resource owners (the bourgeoisie), even when well-meaning, are bound by rules external to their wills and *must* behave accordingly or slip into the ranks of the proletariat. Capital owners and workers who fail to maximize profit in a competitive world will be destroyed. Both are prisoners of the system. Indeed, Marx sees the capitalist as a victim, if a less suffering one than the worker, of the alienation caused by capitalism.

To protect such a system, all other institutions must be brought into harmony with it. Children must be taught that they live in the best of all possible worlds and they should accept what they cannot change. Religion renders unto Caesar that which is his. God mops up the mess at the end of our lives. If we are not wealthy, we must blame ourselves—our liberal politics tells us that we are not using our freedom well.

A Positive Look at Marxism

Placing Marxism in its best light, we can say that the Marxist System has great faith in human will. Marx sees life as a dynamic process in continuous flux. People change and are changed by circumstances. They are free, but not entirely. Marx is a moral man. He is concerned with the quality of life. He is appalled by the misery and degradation he sees around him and wants to change all that. He believes that through a scientific analysis of the way life or history proceeds, people can understand the forces that mold them. Armed with that understanding, when the time is right, they can act. Above all, Marx believes that humankind can take its fate into its own hands. He sees all life as interconnected, so by grasping the essential level of power—the economy—one can control all else. He believes one must actually change society itself rather than hope (with utopian reformers) to build on the altruism of its members.

Marx's goals are humane. True morality can be established by the application of science to human affairs. He believes that ending the alienation of humankind from nature and from its essential self is the achievable end product of the historical process. Finally he believes that people can be free, free from what Marx calls "forced labor," of work necessary to live, so that work takes its rightful place as the natural creative dimension of human existence.

6

The Plan of the Book

The aim of the book is to show how all the elements in Marx's thought come together in a unified whole in which the linchpin is Hegel's theory of human progress, the dialectical process that carries human understanding or "self-awareness" to higher and higher planes. In Hegel's dialectical process, Marx discovers the secret of how society evolves from lower to higher forms of development and ultimately brings humans to a high state of material well-being and moral excellence. How Marx converts Hegel's "idealism" to "dialectical materialism" is explained in chapter 2.

Chapter 3 records Marx's use of dialectical materialism to move his argument away from philosophy and on to economics. The tragedy of "alienation" is central to the process. Economic factors that inhere in the human condition and are exacerbated by social relationships result in this tragedy of alienation, which becomes the motive force for economic and social change in history.

The history of alienation is the history of the breakup of all prior political and social organizations. For Marx it becomes inescapable that until the causes of human alienation are eliminated, the relationships among people will remain poisoned and there will be attendant social disruption. Chapter 4 explores the concept of alienation as a way of understanding history.

Marx's insight with respect to the processes of social change is the standpoint from which he criticizes the response of others concerned with the misery that they see all about them. Marx thinks that most of those who peddle nostrums for social ills are little better than medicine men who do not understand the causes of the diseases they purport to treat. He uses the derogatory term "utopian" for those socialists who, although well-meaning, can do no good for the world because they do not understand it. Chapter 5 presents Marx's critique of the various socialisms of his day.

Marx sees human institutions and behavior as being deeply rooted in the material world. Chapter 6 delves into what that means in terms of social change. In a brief historical review, I consider Marx's demonstration of how underlying changes in the social structure, working through the dialectical process, have caused social institutions to evolve. I also consider his argument that the "relations of production," a basically economic concept, influence, even determine, all other social relationships and tend to obscure the realities of human interaction that lie behind them. With this chapter the foundations of the Marxist system are completely accounted for. The standpoint from which Marx analyzes capitalism is fully set and the moral issue is already clear. Social and economic relationships in most societies are exploitative and cause alienation.

In chapter 7 Marx's sociology, which is primarily his theory of classes, is used to show how, specifically in capitalism, the power of the ruling elite, the property-owning bourgeoisie, is used to subjugate workers. Chapter 8 describes Marx's theory of how the political, religious, and value systems of capitalism are used to create a state and a belief system powerful enough to keep workers from perceiving their own problems or, in the event that they do, to keep them in check.

Chapters 9 and 10 relate to Marx's economics. Nothing that has been said until now shows how the economic system, even the extant capitalist system, is subject to the same laws of motion as all preceding systems. Marx, as shown in these two chapters, sets out to show how capitalism actually works and why its internal dynamics operate according to the dialectical process and will eventually self-destruct.

Chapter 11 is the epilogue to the review of the Marxist system. Here we see how out of the debris of fallen capitalism arises a new society worthy of humankind. "History" comes to an end with the advent of communism.

The reader who wishes to remain uncorrupted by the author's own opinion is invited to skip chapter 12 with its brief evaluation of Marxism. The intent of the chapter is not to undercut Marx but rather to raise some questions, many of which remain unsettled, as to Marx's method of analysis and some of the assumptions that he makes in order to complete his systematic analysis of capitalism and its civilization. It is in this chapter that I ask whether Marxism, the policy, has failed because Marxism, the theory, is faulty or whether Marxism has been abused by its adherents. Also addressed is the question of the future of Marxism, the theory, in face of the failure of so-called Marxist policy.

Finally, the reader may wish to look at chapters 13 and 14 for a brief synopsis of Marx's eventful and tragic life. It was a remarkable life, and one that arouses one's curiosity as to how a mid-European immigrant to Britain, a country with a culture so different from his own, a poor and personally disputatious man, without a political base, could have influenced the world so profoundly and permanently by the force of his personality and genius.

CHAPTER 2

HEGEL AND FEUERBACH

Unlike England and France, Germany was brushed only lightly by the Enlightenment. The German Enlightenment during the eighteenth century had no scientific tradition similar to that of those nations, therefore no sense of the indivisibility and universality of the laws governing the universe, society, and individual lives. If the French and British thinkers of that century believed that scientific study could uncover the universal laws that governed the natural universe in which societies and individuals should, for their own benefit, live in harmony, German philosophers saw no such possibility. For them history was a series of unique social events, each one requiring its own interpretation. Nevertheless, the German philosophic stance was optimistic. Although no all-inclusive theory of the natural and social universe existed, there was general confidence that in the long run Germans would be set free of tyrannical rule and would live as citizens in a great German state.

The nationalist orientation of German philosophy appears to have been related to the political fragmentation of Germany that was in turn partly responsible for the relative isolation of German intellectual life from that of the rest of Europe until the mid-eighteenth century. German national aspirations seemed to find their expression only in the work of intellectuals living in universities dotted around Germany.

If Enlightenment theorists in England and France saw human salvation in the working out of natural law, their German counterparts believed in the progress of history. Whereas natural-law theorists saw in Newton's unified and predictable universe rules that emphasized the "inalienable rights" of individuals, even against the purposes of the state, German national experience permitted no such fundamental political theorizing. Certainly radical individualism could not emerge in a Germany consisting of a profusion of small despotic states prior to unification in 1871. If the Enlightenment relegated God to the end of the universe, as its distant "author" rather than an actual participant,

German pietism, particularly Lutheranism, kept deism and other heterodox views at bay.

Frederick the Great (1712-86) established the Leibniz Academy in Berlin, where European philosophers and scientists gathered. As a consequence, beliefs that had long been held in Western countries, including bourgeois individualism and optimism, began to spread in Germany. Particular centers of Enlightenment thought developed in universities such as those in Göttingen and Berlin. But the German Enlightenment was essentially conservative. Although upholding the dignity of all humans, it celebrated the "German soul." Whereas the Enlightenment in the West was a universal doctrine embracing the human race, the German tradition was bounded by the longing for nationality.

Immanuel Kant (1724-1804) was one of the greatest philosophers and most perceptive critics of the Enlightenment. His views reflected his distrust of Enlightenment assumptions—the unity of all knowledge, the essential goodness of human nature, and the benevolence of the natural world. He rejected the optimistic conviction of the inevitability of progress, and he rejected not only the religious basis of ethics but also utilitarianism and justifications of human behavior on other grounds, such as human happiness.

Kant's legacy was ambiguous. Kant had taken the world as it was, eschewing a metaphysical system that transcended everyday experience, and providing instead a clearly defined conception of how the world ought to work and did in fact work. But his rejection of Enlightenment assumptions left his followers without adequate theories of man, God, and nature.

By the beginning of the nineteenth century the Enlightenment in Germany had run its course. The Terror in France had revealed the evil side of attempting to order the world according to some concept of rational order. And the close of the Napoleonic wars had seen the end of liberalism and a return to absolutism on the continent of Europe.

In Germany, the search for a metaphysics of reality continued. And it was Hegel who constructed the intellectual system that was to alter the history of the world for most of the twentieth century.

Hegel, in the tradition of German historicism, developed a metaphysics that seemed to Marx to answer all the questions that Kant had left unaddressed. It is Hegel's holistic theory of the progress of history that underlies the Marxist System.

From Hegel to Marx

Marx derives his theory of social change from Georg Wilhelm Friedrich Hegel (1770-1831) and Ludwig Andreas Feuerbach (1804-1872). As a young man, Marx was enthralled with Hegel, as were many of his intellectual contemporaries in Germany.

It would not be an exaggeration to say that Hegel was the foremost philosopher in the Germany of the 1830s and 1840s. Often, however, his admirers did not care for the conservative conclusions Hegel drew from his philosophy. And, as it happened, radical political conclusions were as easily derived from it as conservative ones. By 1842 the Young Hegelian school, of which Marx was a part, drew left-wing political conclusions from Hegel by focusing on his method rather than his content.

Hegel was staunchly conservative. Indeed, he was a supporter of Frederick William III, king of the repressive Prussian state. Hegel's philosophy led him to acceptance of that state both because it "existed" and was therefore "necessary," logically and historically, and because it seemed to have achieved that pinnacle of social organization toward which history pointed. Not surprisingly, given such support, Hegel was accepted as the philosopher laureate of the state and was honored accordingly.

Marx accepts Hegel's conception of the method by which the state (and humankind) achieve self-realization, but comes to it from another direction. Denying what will be explained as Hegelian "idealism," or, more literally, "ideaism," in favor of Feuerbach's "materialism," Marx says that he "turns Hegel off his head," still using much of Hegel's method. Marx remains a Hegelian, but a materialist rather than an idealist. This distinction was crucial to his policy recommendations, though not to his view of how the world was likely to develop and where history was taking it. Marx turns from contemplating the external world and the way it works to improve humankind's self-awareness, to action upon a "sensible," that is, material or real, world to change it toward the direction in which history is pointing. Hegel and Marx agree that this direction is toward the perfection of the social order and the consequent perfection of human beings. I next consider Marx's criticism of Hegel and his acceptance and criticism of Feuerbach and finally attempt to uncover Marx's own world view.

Hegel and the Question of Philosophy

Engels writes: "The great basic question of all philosophy . . . is that concerning the relation of thinking and being. . . . [Being] ignorant of the structure of their own bodies . . . [people] came to believe that their thinking and sensations were not activities of their bodies, but of a distinct soul which inhabits the body and leaves it at death."[1] This, says Engels, is the issue of the relationship between spirit and nature. The question is, Is there a soul separate from the body? Philosophers who asserted that God created the world became the school of idealists. Those who asserted the primacy of nature (or the body) belong to various schools of "materialism" (or as we say today, realism). Engels says that the other side of the issue of thinking and being is "In what relation do our thoughts about the world surrounding us stand to this world itself?" Are our ideas about the world a correct reflection of reality? Hegel says yes. We understand the world through our thought process and gradually learn to understand it more and more (over historical time) until we realize the "absolute idea," which has existed from eternity, before the world and independent of it.

An individual starts at the lowest level of self-understanding—then through the historical process, the logic by which history moves forward, he or she reaches continually higher states of self-awareness.

Each society, according to Engels's understanding of Hegel, if it exists for a length of time, is "real" or "true" as it exists. Truth is therefore not an absolute category "to be learned by heart" dogmatically, but is true for a time. The process of history is always upward; one's understanding of oneself and the world is always improving in the movement of an idea toward freedom—until in the end, there is achieved a perfect society with people who completely understand themselves. Men and women and society reach the "absolute." In a perfect world humankind becomes God. At that point, history comes to an end.

Each stage of human history is "true" with a small *t,* and is therefore necessary (if it survives a while). With this in mind, Hegel justified Prussian repressiveness under Frederick William III. But societies carry the seeds of their own destruction, their own internal contradictions. In human terms, human understanding or self-knowledge is also self-contradictory or self-alienating. (Alienation is important in Marxism, as we see in the next chapter.) The process by which a "reality," a necessary historical point in time of a given society, dissolves itself into the next higher stage of development (of human self-awareness) is called the dialectic process, the process that ends for Hegel in the "absolute idea" at the end of history.

The dialectic process can be explained this way: There exists a reality or truth or necessary existing state of the world or state of human self-understanding. This is the *thesis.* But inside each thesis (or existing reality, truth, state of human understanding, etc.) exists its *antithesis.* They struggle. Out of this struggle emerges a *synthesis* (a new thesis, affirmation, truth, or state of self-awareness), which is "higher," that is, closer to the "absolute idea," than the previous state. The higher synthesis is an *aufhebung,* a new level that contains and restructures the previous level.

Hegel's concept of logic is simply that ideas are related to one another by rules, the same rules that relate real-world events to one another. Dialectic is thus a kind of logic in action with the real world.

The main argument Marx and Engels had with Hegel can be summarized this way: Human history is understood by the mind. Although it is clear to the Marxist that the human mind must understand what is happening in the natural world, the mind itself is a part of the natural or real world. That we understand with our minds does not make history "happen" there, as Hegel seems to be saying. History happens in the real material world.

Feuerbach's Contribution

Marx, who was a Hegelian in his early years, was strongly influenced by another Young Hegelian, Ludwig Feuerbach, whose materialism provided a philosophic base for challenging both the Hegelian doctrine of idealism and his "essentialism," the view of the existence of the "absolute idea" and "logical categories" before the world existed. Only one idea of Feuerbach's, but the central one, was congenial to Marx. It is that "the material, sensuously perceptible world to which we ourselves belong is the only reality; and that our consciousness and thinking, however suprasensuous they may seem, are the product of a material, bodily organ, the brain."[2]

Feuerbach's *Essence of Christianity* substitutes materialism for Hegelian idealism. Engels explains that Feuerbach shows that "nature exists independently of all philosophy."[3] Human beings are products of nature. Engels explains why nothing exists outside of nature: "Our religious fantasies . . . are only the fantastic reflection of our own essence."[4] Though Feuerbach "discarded" Hegelianism, "Hegelianism could not be simply ignored, it had to be reincarnated in a different form." That is, its treatment of Idea as the originating force was rejected, but the methodology, which Marx and Engels found valuable, "had to be saved."

Beyond the insight provided by Feuerbach that "matter is not a product of mind, but mind itself is merely the highest product of matter,"[5] Engels finds his materialism to be inadequate. Feuerbach's contribution to philosophy was to settle the mind-matter issue squarely in favor of matter. But his understanding of "matter" was insufficient. The materialism of the eighteenth century continues to exist today and is predominantly mechanical, says Engels.[6] In the natural sciences only the mechanics of gravity were then understood. Nature was in eternal motion, turning in circles but never developing, never changing form nor able to create new forms.

In short, eighteenth-century materialism was antievolutionary as well as antidialectical. Feuerbach, who "rusticated" in a little German village most of his life, never knew Charles Darwin. Feuerbach believed that Hegel's dialectical process was to be saved; his historical process had to be preserved. Feuerbach shared with Hegel his concept of the logic of historical processes, which in Marx's view could not move the world forward because only ideas, not material things, changed. Also Feuerbach was, in Engels's view, an idealist. He believed that love emancipated mankind. Religion is to be perfected, not abolished, and in his new religion sexual love becomes one of the highest experiences .[7]

Feuerbach Compared with Hegel

According to Engels, Feuerbach, like Hegel, is basically an idealist. For all of his talk of God as being only a "fantastic reflection, a mirror image of man," God is in the end an abstract idea and man is not a real human being. As soon as Feuerbach ceases discussing sexual relations, he is dealing abstractly. Even then his only real concern is with morality.

Hegel's understanding of ethical matters is far richer than Feuerbach's. According to Engels, Hegel's doctrine of moral conduct, his philosophy of the right, is based on abstract topics, morality and social ethics. His social ethics is concerned with the family, civil society, and the state. He also treats the law, economy, and politics. Hegel, the idealist, discusses the philosophy of the right *realistically*, although his categories appear abstract. With Feuerbach, the realist, it is the reverse, says Engels. Whereas he takes "man" as his starting place, he makes absolutely no reference to the world in which man lives. Hence he remains abstract. "For this man is not born of women; he issues, as from a chrysalis, from the god of the monotheistic religions. Of sociology he knows nothing."[8]

Hegel writes: "One believes [that] one is saying something great . . . if one says that man is naturally good, but one says something far greater when one says man is naturally evil!"[9] Feuerbach, on the other hand, never investigates moral evil. He lacks any sense of history and is capable of such a sterile dictum as the following: "Man as he sprang originally from nature was only a mere creature of nature, not a man. Man is a product of man, of culture, of history."[10] For Hegel, evil is a motive force in history. To most people any advance in human affairs appears as a sacrilege against things hallowed, a rebellion against moribund things sanctified by custom. Yet it is just this antagonism in its form of class conflict that propels history. Of this Feuerbach says nothing.

What Feuerbach can teach us about morals is meager, beginning with his assumption that since the urge to happiness is innate, happiness must be the basis of all morality. Engels explains that man, for Feuerbach, has an innate urge to happiness subject to a "double correction." The natural consequences of our actions are the corrections. "After the debauch comes the blues, and habitual excess is followed by illness." Second, there can be social consequences of the urge to achieve happiness. If, in pursuing one's own happiness one doesn't "respect the similar urge" in others, they will defend themselves. The ideal is "rational self-restraint" and love—"again and again love."[11]

Feuerbach's urge to happiness has no real moral content. In his theory of morals, "the Stock Exchange is the highest temple of moral conduct, provided only that one always speculates right . . . if he loses his money, his action is *ipso facto* proved to have been unethical [and he has been] given the punishment he deserves."[12]

Feuerbach's morality is designed to suit all periods, profiles, and conditions, and is therefore useless. Engels argues that Feuerbach's morality is as powerless as Kant's concept of the categorical imperative to affect the real world, because it is abstract and relates to no real thing in particular. Engels reasserts his belief, derived from Hegel, that, "in reality every class, even every profession, has its own morality, and even this it violates whenever it can do so with impunity." Engels says that Feuerbach's love, "which is to unite all, manifests itself in wars, altercations, lawsuits, domestic brawls, divorces, and every possible exploitation of one by another."[13]

Marx on Hegel

Engels complains that although Feuerbach's concept of man and nature as material objects was powerful, he never used it to understand real nature or real man. In 1845, in his *The Holy Family,* Marx went beyond Feuerbach, replacing his "cult" of abstract man in his new religion with the "science of real men and of their historical development," as Engels put it.

"Hegel was not simply put aside." Marx "started out from his [Hegel's] revolutionary side [and] from the dialectic method."[14] He believed the Hegelian form of dialectic method was unusable because nothing changes in the real world. All that develops dialectically in Hegelian thought is the "absolute concept," which for Hegel exists from eternity, and is the "actual living soul of the whole existing world." The real world is left unchanged.

Therefore, the dialectic process in nature and history, moving "from lower to higher," with intervening zigzag movements and temporary retrogressions, is, in Hegel's thought, simply the self-propelled movement of the "absolute concept", an abstract idea that has existed forever and that continues to travel to who knows where. Hegel argues that all events are independent of a thinking human brain. Marx, understanding the same events materialistically, sees concepts in his head as real things rather than as images. Ideas cannot exist abstractly, unconnected to human consciousness.

For Marx dialectics became the science of the laws of general motion, both of the external world and human thought. Both sets of laws have identical reality but differ in their expression "insofar as the human mind can apply them consciously." These same laws assert themselves in nature "in the form of external necessity," looking like a series of random accidents. The dialectic of concepts is merely the conscious reflex of dialectic motion in the real world. In this way Hegel's idealism is inverted and becomes in Marx's hand materialism.

The basic thought of the dialectic of materialism is that the world is not a complex of preexisting things but "a complex of *processes,* in which apparently stable things undergo continuous change, coming into being and passing away, seemingly accidentally, sometimes appearing temporarily to be retrogressive, but in the end showing itself to have been a progressive development. The dialectic process is real; our minds reflect its reality. It is complex, seemingly unconnected, drifting, and sometimes going backward, but in the end always in an upward or improved direction. Necessity is composed of sheer accidents . . . the so-called accidental is the form behind which necessity hides itself."[15]

Theses on Feuerbach

Marx, in his *Theses on Feuerbach,* stresses the importance of human action in moving history. Feuerbach's materialism was inadequate; he was an idealist in social theory. Marx believes that the reality or nonreality of thinking as a subject of intellectual discussion is an arid distinction. What counts is practice—human participation in human affairs. Action renders debate about reality "scholastic" (THESIS II).

The materialist doctrine that people are both products of circumstances and can change circumstances describes a dualism, a simultaneous and mutual interaction of man and society. This reciprocating activity can only be understood as a function of continuous revolution (THESIS III).

The most that can be said about what Marx calls contemplative (nonfunctioning) materialism is that it does not understand practical activity. Individuals are seen as single unattached beings, separate from civil society. People cannot be separate from the society of which they are a part. As part of that society they work to change themselves and society at the same time (THESIS IX).

Philosophers have only a limited role to play. They interpret the world as spectators. The real point is to change it (THESIS XI).[16]

Summary

To understand Marxism, it is necessary to understand what Marx called the

"German ideology." That ideology was rooted in German political and intellectual history. It was antitheoretical in the sense of being antirationalistic. It tended to examine history as a set of unique human experiences, essentially those experiences in Germany. Hegel, Germany's greatest speculative philosopher, is in the tradition of those who put the German experience into a comprehensive metaphysical system that took the form that has been described as idealism.

Marx and Engels are Hegelian. Feuerbach had already transformed Hegelian idealism into materialism, leaving to Marx only to add that nature is real and that the brain that transmits ideas about the world around us is part of nature, too. This, then, denies the dualism in much speculative philosophy regarding the mind and soul as separate from body or nature and undercuts the idea of personal creation and, presumably, the concept of a special preordained destiny for the world and humankind. Marx and Engels deny the former, but appear to hold on to the latter. "History" replaces God as author of the universe. The destiny of humans is their ultimate perfection. In this respect they are still Hegelians.

In chapter 3 we turn to one of the central concepts that Marx derived from Hegel, the concept of alienation. Alienation is the source of human conflict, a central consequence of capitalism. It is both the cause of human degradation and the hope for the ultimate redemption of the human race. The concept of alienation is, therefore, basic to the Marxist System.

CHAPTER 3

THE THEORY OF ALIENATION

Marx's theory of alienation is a direct descendant of Hegelian idealism and closely linked to the romantic German philosophic tradition. In the romantic view, alienation is a wholly subjective phenomenon. The individual is unable to live with inner tranquillity in society. Alienation, for Marx, is caused by the worker's separation from that which he has produced. Indeed, the individual is enslaved by that which he has created. Objects that humans create take on lives of their own. They, like Frankenstein's monster, are reified. The creator is destroyed by a monster of his own making. In this chapter I show how Marx's theory of alienation, derived from Hegel, changes in Marx's hands from philosophy into economics.

Hegelian philosophy, which embodies the traditional Christian belief in the duality of body and soul, in Marx's hands subscribes to the duality of man and nature. Marx shifts Hegel's idea from a world of the mind to a world of material things. Philosophy is transformed into economics.

Marx's theory of alienation leads directly to his contention that society must create the conditions in which the true (essential) self can be fully realized. Indeed, Marxism argues that humans are incapable of adjusting to changing social conditions and, for that reason, must make a Herculean effort to restructure society to fit human needs. At the end of this chapter I discuss a more recent view of alienation for purposes of clarifying some of the issues surrounding that concept.

Hegel's Alienation and
the Dialectical Process

Hegel was, in philosophic language, an essentialist, holding that human beings have an essence that is malleable. That is, it can be renewed and improved over time. The history of human freedom is the history of the struggle of people, of their essences, to become perfect. And this takes place in a real world in which human beings have material bodies.

Religious people would argue that the body is the temporary house of the soul; the body turns to dust, and the soul continues on. Hegel uses the term "self-consciousness" as religious persons use the term soul. Humans, for Hegel, are in a condition of "alienated self-consciousness." That is, their bodies and souls are separated. To be so separated is to be alienated. Marx denies the duality of body and soul and argues that the conflict Hegel sees between the two is nothing more than the conflict between people's "true" selves and their actual behavior, a conflict that is created in the real world by the real material conditions under which people live.

Hegel is concerned with reuniting body and soul. But Marx, in seeking to overcome alienation, is not reuniting body and soul. They were never separated, he maintains; the very concept is erroneous. People are born with a true and good human nature that becomes corrupted by the imperfections of the real world. The movement of history is toward helping people achieve their full human potential in the material world. And that conception is the hallmark of Marx's materialism as contrasted with Hegel's idealism. When alienation is overcome through history, the material world is made perfect, thus allowing people to become perfect. Human happiness and fullest self-development then become realities.

The nub of Marx's method is found in his adaptation of Hegel's solution to the problem of overcoming alienation. For Hegel, alienation is overcome in historical time through the dialectical *process*. He sees the spiritual self as compelled by inner necessity to overcome alienation. For Marx, the condition of alienation is so irritating that mechanisms develop to assuage the discomfort. For Marx there is strong human motivation for social change to overcome alienation, whereas for Hegel "history" has the purpose of overcoming alienation so as to make humans at one with God.

The issue for Hegel, according to Marx in the *Economic and Philosophic Manuscripts of 1844*, "is to surmount the object of consciousness." In the complex language of Hegel, "object" means the "real" or "material" world or person. So it is the real world, which contains the human body in which the "soul" resides, that has to be overcome. There exists for Hegel an essential person, a spiritual being that was not created when the human body and the physical world were created, that has existed for all eternity. The words "soul" or "self-conscious being" can be used to describe Hegel's conception of the human essence.

For Hegel, the condition of alienation occurs because the "soul" of a human being is housed in a material body. There is also a conflict between events that occur in the larger material world and those that take place in the mind. More than that, since all that we know about the material world can be known only in the mind, the mind can be said to *create* the real world. The real world is an extension of the mind. Marx argues conversely, as we will see, that the real world creates the mind. However, this duality of body and soul, the world of the human spirit and the material world, creates an antagonism, alienation, "estrangement"—the condition to be overcome. The body can be said to be "alien" to the soul. The problem is to reunite them. To Hegel's thinking the need is to "annul estrangement [and wipe out] objectivity [the objective world and the material body] as well. Man . . . is regarded as a nonobjective, spiritual being."[1]

The *dialectical* process is the process of interaction between what goes on in the mind and what goes on in the material world. The mind creates matter, its own contradiction (or, in Hegel's language, creates its own *negation*). Presumably uncomfortable with a contradiction within itself, it takes back into itself what it has created to negate the negation. More simply, the mind creates an objective world, the one we see around us, but is uncomfortable with it because the mind is always uncomfortable with a material reality outside of itself. Or, realizing that what it has created is still imperfect, the mind reabsorbs the real world and creates another one which, though still unsatisfactory, is "better." Out of the negation of the negation comes a new "synthesis," a new real world on a higher plane.

"History" is the dialectical process, Hegel asserts. Each new synthesis is on a higher, more spiritual plane. It "supersedes" its predecessor. Humans are more "self-conscious," more self-aware with each new historical condition. History is therefore evolutionary and progressive. The real world gets better; the mind likes its product better. As is not the case with the French materialists whom we meet in chapter 5, history has a direction and purpose which, for Hegel, is to reunite the body with the spirit, thereby arriving at the only condition in which there exists no alienation. History, as Hegel sees it, is a journey to understanding, understanding oneself, and becoming more and more perfect or self-aware, until one is reunited with God.

The art of superseding is the building of thought upon thought. The real world is created as the negation of the thought in order to be superseded so that thought can continue its upward movement to the absolute idea (God). The whole purpose of the exercise is to raise the level of self-consciousness to its full awareness of itself, which is God. Man becomes God. God becomes fully realized.[2]

Marx, using Hegelian categories, provides historical examples to show that human history is one of progress from lower to higher civilizations. Because Hegel's scheme depends upon what Marx accepts to be the case, that history does indeed have purpose and direction, Marx is able to adapt the dialectic to his own purposes.

Actual world history from the "barbaric" times to the present capitalist-dominated world, according to Marx, provides an example of how, for Hegel, an "idea" evolves over time. The human mind creates, in a manner of speaking, a primitive or "barbaric" tribal society. That society contains the negation of the tribal idea. The negation may be, for instance, a sudden growth of population, making the organization nonviable. That negation, imperfect and unsustainable tribal form, is "taken back" into the mind or consciousness of people, who then create in their minds new forms, which embody useful elements of the tribal world and until that time unknown forms. This synthesis of old and new appears in history, say, as feudalism. But feudalism, too, has its contradictions. Feudalism is in some senses "superior" to tribalism but yet imperfect. In the same way the idea of capitalism appears first in abstract form and then comes to life as capitalism in real-life form. Each historical world form is superseded by another as the dialectical process works itself out.

Marx's Critique of Hegel

Marx, as we know, accepts Hegel's dialectic method as a way of understanding the process of social change. But he criticizes Hegel's idealism as being devoid of real content—it is an abstract idea about life, not life itself. Therefore, the dialectic process of change in Hegel's hands is no more than the process by which one abstract idea is converted into another without influence on what happens in the real world. Abstract ideas are capable only of creating other abstract ideas. To negate an idea and to replace it with another idea is but an *abstract* and *empty* form of any real living act.[3] The real world changes dialectically. Hegel's abstract world, the world as seen by philosophers as an "idea," changes not at all.

For Hegel, Marx complains, the history of mankind becomes the history of an abstract spirit of mankind, "a spirit beyond man."[4] Hegel claims that the absolute spirit in history treats mass (or the real world) as material that finds its true expression in philosophy. Marx says that a philosopher participates in history as an observer. He looks backward on what has happened, whereas real history is accomplished by the Absolute Spirit *unconsciously*. All the philosopher provides us with, in terms of an understanding of what has happened, is the opinion or conception of the philosopher, who was not around, or who is not really aware of what was happening. How can the World Spirit become conscious of itself if the necessary interpreter was simply not part of the process, was not even "there" to interpret the world?

For Hegel, says Marx, the life process goes on in the human brain. The thinking process called "the Idea" is for Hegel an independent subject. The brain records only a mirror image of the world. Marx maintains that the real world is external to the brain: "With me, on the contrary, the ideal is nothing else than the material world reflected by the human mind, and translated into forms of thought."[5]

Marx on Alienation

The creation of objective consciousness (the real human being) by the self-conscious (the essence of the human being) is the language Hegel uses in talking about self-alienation, or the way separation of mind and body occurs. The whole dialectical process of surmounting objective consciousness through understanding (or becoming self-aware) is a process by which alienation is overcome. The process of "superseding," Hegel teaches, is the way in which alienation is overcome by stages so that when awareness is "absolute" (one understands all), one becomes God; the self is reunited into a single abstract being. Self-alienation has been overcome.

Marx converts Hegelian alienation into an alienation in which the dualism of human being and spirit shifts to another dualism, of human being and the world. There remains for Marx an essential person who is incomplete because he is separated (estranged, alienated) by the world of work (broadly speaking) from his true self. As we see in chapter 4, in states of savagery or barbarism, Marx argues that an individual lives harmoniously with himself or herself, his or her fellows, and the natural world. It is only in the contemporary, more recently developed, capitalist world that humans are alienated.

Marx disdains the theory that the origin of alienation can be traced to prehistory. For him alienation is not necessarily a condition of human existence. Historically it comes into being when the division of labor appears and exchange (for money) takes place. The division of labor is the root cause of alienation. The division of labor and connected exchange are converted to economic growth, society becoming richer in goods. It is then, says Marx, that "the *increasing value* of the world of things proceeds in direct proportion to the *devaluation* of the world of men. Labor produces not only commodities: it produces itself and the workers as a *commodity*—and does so in the proportion in which it produces commodities generally."[6]

The commodity produced "confronts" labor as "*something* alien, as a *power independent* of the producer." Labor has been congealed as an object. "The material thing is nothing but the objectification of labor." It appears as a "*loss of reality*," "loss of object," "object bondage." Objectification is so much the loss of reality that the worker may starve to death. He is robbed of the object most necessary to his life. Labor becomes an object outside the worker (alien to himself) to such a degree that the worker loses power over his or her own labor, or "his labor becomes a power on its own confronting him."[7] The estrangement of this object of labor is merely "summarized in the estrangement, the alienation, in the activity of labor itself."

When labor is external to the worker, he or she does not freely develop mental and physical energy. The worker stagnates in mind and body, feels best when not working. Therefore, work is not joyful and spontaneous; it is coerced. When at the workplace, labor is not undertaken to satisfy the worker's needs but to satisfy the needs of others. When one works for another person, not for oneself, the worker feels like an animal, laboring just to satisfy human functions of eating, dressing, dwelling, and procreating, and doing nothing purely human.[8]

To summarize thus far: There are several aspects of human estrangement. First is alienation of the object of work: The product has a power over the person. Second is the relationship of the laborer to the act of working. The activity does not belong to the worker, and thus "working is a form of suffering." The worker's own physical and mental life is turned against him. The second is that of self-estrangement, estrangement from one's own nature.

The third aspect of estrangement is from nature. Man is a "species-being," a life form of its own, but also part of nature, nourished by nature, needing nature to live—to eat, to clothe himself, to dwell. Nature is man's inorganic body. But man is not inorganic nature, even though he lives off nature—man and nature are linked.

The estrangement of man from nature and himself (his productive functions, his life activity) estranges the species from the individual. As man is estranged from himself, he is estranged from nature and thus from his species-being, his special characteristic as a human being. When humans are estranged from their "species-being," they can no longer be distinguished from animals. For a man to be human, his activities involve will and consciousness. Human activity is free activity.

A consequence of the estrangement from nature and from the "species-being" is that human beings are estranged from one another. Just as persons are confronted by alienated work, they are confronted by other people. Each person holds the other person's labor as the object of his or her labor (rather than an extension of the human activity of another individual). Each individual sees every other individual from the standpoint of the position in which the worker sees himself or herself. (He may see one as a rival, a competitor, or an owner—generally with hostility.)

Private property has a symbiotic relationship with estranged labor. Private property, a creation of human labor, is, in actuality, alienated labor (alien to the laborer, standing outside it) and is the source of conflict between laborer and capitalist. Thus yet another "estrangement" is created. Worker is estranged from nonworker, the capitalist, who "owns" the labor embodied in private property.

Alienation and Political Economy

As early as the *Economic and Philosophic Manuscripts of 1844*, Marx applies his concept of alienation to a critical review of the "classical" economics widely accepted in the first half of the nineteenth century, which was taught and practiced by Adam Smith, David Ricardo, and John Stuart Mill.

"Modern" political economy, according to Marx, accepts the interrelationship of the division of labor and the accumulation of wealth. The division of labor is necessary for the accumulation of wealth. Private property "left to itself [freed from medieval restrictions on use and sale] can produce the most useful and comprehensive division of labor." Smith argues that "division of labor bestows on labor infinite production capacity . . . which stems from the *propensity to exchange and barter*, a specific human propensity." Marx denies these anthropomorphic propensities. "The motive in exchange is not *humanity* but *egotism*."[9] The development of highly specialized human beings is not the cause but the effect of the division of labor. The diversity of talent is made useful only in a system where exchange exists. The division of labor goes forward limited by the extent of exchange, by the scope of the market. "In advanced conditions, every man is a merchant, and society is a commercial society."[10] (Adam Smith is virtually plagiarized here—but not in homage.)

The division of labor and exchange are "*perceptibly alienated* expressions of human *activity*." To assert that the division of labor and exchange is contingent on private property is to say that labor is the essence of private property. The fact that the division of labor and exchange are creatures of private property proves that human life requires private property for its realization and that human life these days requires the supremacy of private property. Marx is saying that the alienated form requires the institution of private property. Therefore, to remove alienation, private property must also disappear.

Marx has much more to say about the importance of private property in the issue of alienation. The alienated worker works not for himself or herself but for the capitalist "or whatever one chooses to call the master of labor. Private property is thus the product, the result, the necessary consequence, of alienated labor, of the external relation of the worker to nature (land) and to himself." *Private property* is not the source of *alienated labor*, it is the consequence. If the root cause of alienation is the division of labor, private property is its symptom. Marx's ultimate solution to alienation is to abolish the division of labor and, by inference, private property.

The relationship of labor to capital is this: Capital is stored-up living labor. The worker is living capital "and therefore a capital *with needs.*" Capital, when not working, loses its interest (earns no interest) and therefore its livelihood. The value of the worker, as capital, fluctuates with demand and supply like a commodity. The worker's *life* is looked upon as a commodity. The worker's human qualities exist only as they "exist for capital alien to him." The worker produces capital, and capital produces the worker. The worker is no longer a human being but is a commodity who "can go and bury himself, starve to death, etc."

The worker is needed, so he must be maintained *while he is working, to prevent the race of laborers from dying out.* Maintaining the worker has the same significance as maintaining a piece of equipment, similar to "oil which is applied to the wheels to keep them turning." English political economists David Ricardo and James Mill could show with a clear sense of logic that what was important was that wages and interest were competitors for income. Squeezing money from the consumer was never the issue, but squeezing money from one another was the normal relationship. The capitalist could gain only at the expense of labor. National income was made of two parts, interest and wages. If workers profited by high wages, capitalists suffered. According to the analysis of political economists, production was an impersonal activity. A human being was an abstract essence, "a mere workman"—an "input," we would say—to be utilized or dispensed with according to the needs of the economy. Worker as human being has no place in the analysis of political economists.

Another great cornerstone of English political economy was the development of the concept of differential rent. The difference in earnings yielded by the least productive land and the best is called rent. Rent has taken on the same characteristics as interest on capital. The landowner is a capitalist, the tenant farmer the worker. The tenant farmer stands in relation to landlord as worker to capitalist. Landlord and capitalist are at odds with each other, each trying to gain legitimacy in the eyes of society.[11] With the growth of industrialism and the increasing power of the manufacturing class, nineteenth-century political economists took sides with the emerging class against landlords.

Summary

What Marx complains of is the dehumanization of labor (creative, self-aware human activity). Human beings are turned into abstract economic categories;

the worker, no longer a person, is labor receiving wages. Capital is simply congealed human labor appropriated by nonworkers for their own purposes. Capital earns interest, which belongs to the capitalist. Nature becomes land. Land earns rent; the landlord, another nonworker, appropriates the rent. All value is created by labor. In its interest or rent form it is simply stolen by nonworkers. Wages are necessary payments, representing much less than the full value of that which workers create but enough to keep them alive, reproductive, and poor. The institution of private property is simply the historical means by which nature has been stolen from the worker. The division of labor is the "economically rational" way to increase worker output, and exchange is the way human creativity in the form of commodities is objectified as something outside the living being. Marx terms the objectifying of goods and services "commodity fetishism"—giving a life of its own to an object detached from its source.

All of this is a function of alienation, which separates workers from their products, from one another as rivals or antagonists, from capitalist exploiters (who are nonworkers), and from nature by turning land into capital through legalizing its purchase and sale and thereby denying "unauthorized" human beings access to the source of life. The process is degrading and dehumanizing. The task that Hegel envisioned was the reunification of mind and spirit. Marx saw more clearly (he believed) that through revolutionary activity, humans could restore that which had been torn apart, their true humanity. For Hegel, the end result meant growing self-awareness through history; for Marx, it meant reawakening self-awareness in despised and disinherited workers. The purpose of history in Marx's view was to create a communist world where all alienation would come to an end.

Marx posits that alienation is a product of civilization itself. The more complex the organization, the greater the alienation. The division of labor, the root cause of feelings of isolation and loneliness, of powerlessness and meaninglessness, grows along with the progress of civilization. Only a society without a division of labor can overcome alienation. If Marx is correct, no known form of large-scale social organization can restore persons to their full humanity. A society without a division of labor is unimaginable.

Marx's subjective view of alienation takes as a given that humans cannot adjust to the world; the world must adjust to humans. That romantic view of alienation continues to persist among sociologists and anthropologists today. Sometimes the causes of feelings of alienation are thought to be biological. The human nervous system is so structured that its needs cannot be satisfied under modern conditions. Humans need a nurturing environment. They suffer loneliness in large-scale impersonal societies. Others see the fundamental source of alienation as the inability of humans to adjust to the act of being born, the separation of a child from its mother. Still others look to modern social organization, with its large bureaucratic enterprises in which people work at uninteresting or repetitive jobs, as a primary source of alienation. People see a loss of meaning and power in their lives when they do not participate in the selection of the goals toward which they are asked to strive and have no control over the time and pace of their work. The latter group of critics of modern civilization agree with Marx's general position but amend and extend his view.

Some social critics see alienation not as a rebellion against societal norms but as a consequence. Persons may accept the goals and values of society but be unable or not permitted to meet them. Persons who suffer discrimination or who strive without success to achieve accepted standards cannot participate in the rewards of the system. They may feel alienated.

Finally, there are those who simply adjust to their own situation. These realists may try to meet societal norms and fail—due to lack of talent, training, opportunity, or discrimination—and simply carry on. Some people may find themselves in uncongenial jobs or in an environment that is hostile or indifferent. They do not necessarily feel alienated. Whatever the empirical validity of Marx's generalization of the ubiquity of alienation, it is a central idea of the Marxist System.

Marx's concern with the way the economic system alienates humans from their true selves and one another leads to his analysis of how changes, largely from outside the social system in precapitalist times, create the conditions that lead to social change and progress. In chapter 4 we review economic history to show why each economic and social system self-destructs when the conditions of social integration and mutual self-support dissolve, for a variety of reasons, and alienation replaces unity. The emergence of alienation marks the end of the existing system

CHAPTER 4

ECONOMIC SYSTEMS PRIOR TO CAPITALISM

Just as Hegel believed in history as the story of the progress of human self-awareness until God and man were one, so Marx believed in history as the story of human progress until full human perfection is achieved. The achievement of the absolute idea in Hegelian thought was parallel to the Marxist idea of the fully autonomous person. Ever-increasing alienation beset the road to the goal of fully reintegrated personalities. The Christian analogy is obvious. One had first to "fall from grace" (become alienated)—to suffer, in order to be redeemed.

Marx's anthropology is a secular version of sin and redemption. In early human history, "among the ancients," people lived in a kind of Garden of Eden, a place of innocence where people dwelled in harmony with themselves, united with their fellow human beings. Far from inhabiting a Garden of Eden, however, they often lived in squalor. They did not lead happy and productive lives, but at least they were unexploited and not degraded.

Marx describes human history in the following settings: Asiatic, ancient, and feudal. The conditions obtaining in these settings correspond to modes of production that include technology, exchange, and land relationships. Each condition was, for Marx, distinct, and in his writing he moved freely from one to another. Here we record Marx's conception of the reasons for the decline of traditional societies and the rise of the bourgeois condition in which people now live, and how during this process unalienated labor becomes alienated.[1]

In the terminology of economic anthropology, Marx is a member of the "substantivist" school. He saw each historical period as unique, marked by its own values and motivations. Marx did not accept, for instance, the view held by nineteenth- and twentieth-century economists that human wants are limitless. Nor did he believe that profit maximization and cost reduction were central characteristics of all societies, precapitalist or modern.

Marx believed that even though control over the means of exchange was always unequal and rulers "despotic," exploitation did not exist in precapitalist societies. Though inequalities of power were widespread, a fundamental harmony of interests still prevailed. All members of society were unified by tribal, religious, or ethnic bonds. They were fundamentally dedicated to the survival of the group.

Before capitalism, each person had responsibilities and rights as a member of the collectivity. Neither production nor exchange for profit motivated individuals. The group may have been predatory in its interests, trading or waging war as the occasion required. But production was for "use," although surpluses might be exchanged. Exchange was essentially benign and nonexploitative.

Distribution was not "economic"—based on productive contribution or on the relative political strength of factions. In some societies distributive shares were embedded in tradition; where hierarchical organization predominated, for example, position in the social hierarchy determined each person's share. As a generalization, status rather than class determined distributive shares.

For Marx, "economic rationality," along with individualism, a central feature of market societies, is a new phenomenon in human affairs brought about by the dissolution of traditional societies.

Marx argues that labor is alienated when it is free to sell its services in markets and receive wages. The wage laborer works for the sake of earning money in order to survive, not for the enjoyment of commodities that the worker has produced. A free laborer has no obligation to provide services to landlords or to maintain a fixed residence.[2]

For labor to be free, land must also be freely salable on a market. Although throughout history there has always existed "petty ownership," land that individuals can use and control, and property jointly held with others, land is not free unless it can be bought or sold.[3]

But before labor and land can be free, money wealth must be accumulated. Money wealth can develop into capital only when a traditional society is dissolving. Money wealth is at once the cause and the consequence of the dissolution of the existing society in which traditional economic relationships reside. With money wealth individuals can hire labor and secure the ownership of land.

Money wealth and capital are not the same. It is not the accumulation of capital goods—tools, materials, and food—that creates a society dominated by capital and capitalist owners. It is only when a traditional society is dissolving for other reasons that capital equipment is available for purchase. In precapitalist societies capital equipment is common property or is held by individuals for their own use.[4]

Unalienated Labor—The "Ancients"

Such prebourgeois era societies as the Oriental commune contained elements of "petty land ownership" and "communal landed property." In both instances humans enjoy a natural bonding with their land. Because of that bonding, the worker has an objective and independent existence; he is master of his own world. And in a society where free petty land ownership and communally held land dwell side by side, the two forms do not come into conflict with each other.

Individuals in such circumstances are not laborers in the bourgeois sense, but members of a community. They work not to create exchange value but work for the maintenance of the communal body. They trade surpluses for the surpluses of foreign labor.

The loss of a sense of community is a product of history, the history of the transformation of an individual into an alienated laborer. The process occurs when the individual is separated from the source of subsistence, land.

Historically, land as property first appears with the development of a human community either by the spontaneous evolution from family to tribe or by combinations of tribes through intermarriage. Pastoral or migratory life precedes these fixed settlements.

Once settled, the community adapts to its new circumstances in a variety of ways, depending on objective conditions such as climate, geography, physical land characteristics, and the special makeup of the particular tribe. Language develops necessarily.

The relation of people to land in ancient times was that of communal proprietor. They adapted to natural surroundings in accordance with the way they use the soil. In despotic Asiatic forms, the despot stands above the entire community as if he were a sole owner of all property; community members appear to be propertyless and occupiers of the despot's property only with his permission. It appears that the despot appropriates the surplus product of the worker, who is no better than a slave.

Marx claims that these appearances are misleading. The surpluses that are collected by the despot for communal purposes are not derived from exploited labor, nor do they cause alienation. Even though the surplus so collected may take the form of tribute or the form of labor brigades working without pay for the common needs of the group, workers are not being exploited because the product is needed for the provision of collective wants.

Arrangements for the disposal of surplus labor can take two forms. In the first, small communities (towns) band themselves together to work on allotted land, paying part of the surplus to the community or separate towns or to defray communal costs for war or religious worship. This form of community enterprise is rural and is often dominated by lords.

Serfdom also may evolve under these circumstances. Or, as in Mexico, Peru, India, or among the Celts, there may be a single ruler or a group of family heads that represent the community. The function of the leadership may be to provide such publicly consumed products as communal irrigation systems. And the appropriation of surplus labor for such purposes does not result in alienated labor.

The second form of disposal of surplus property is found in cities. Cities do not evolve from clusters of small towns. They are original developments by groups of people who cluster together to achieve mutual ends. Rural areas are economically bound to the cities. Marx sees an intractable conflict of interest between town and country. Cities may be ruled by kings or by military power. Cities, too, are primarily concerned with preservation of the interests of the community as a whole, for redistributing surpluses for communal needs including war. Cities are uniquely suited to organization for war.

In cities the property of the individual is not communal property. The state owns common lands, and private property is separate. There is likely to be social stratification, including higher and lower kinship groups. The city may migrate from place to place, occupying foreign soil. Each new location creates new conditions of labor. Under these conditions private property is likely to develop.

The state is a community made up of private proprietors who freely interact on a basis of equality. It also consists of working landowners and small peasant cultivators who band together to protect their common lands, provide for common needs, and battle for "common glory." The landowner's relation to land is closely associated with his relationship to the community. The landowner not only works as a private proprietor but for the community. His right as to use of the land is conditioned by his obligations as a member of the state. The state is often thought to derive its power from heaven.

The city is the center of state power with rural land as part of its territory. Small agriculture and manufacturing are for domestic consumption. Some wives and daughters spin and weave to maintain their independence. The continued existence of the community depends upon the maintenance of equality among its free and economically independent peasants whose own labor sustains their property. The purpose of work is not to acquire wealth but to provide self-sustenance, to assure reproduction for continuation of the community and of the agricultural workforce. Surplus time and labor belongs to the state for such purposes as war.

In the Germanic tribal setting private property existed side by side with public lands. But private property always meant possession—not ownership as is understood under capitalism. Property was available for use only by members of the community and its use depended upon whether the land was cultivated by a single person or a group of people. The family was an independent unit. Among Asiatics there was no property except communal property. Among Romans there existed both public lands and private landed property. Because both kinds of property existed, the Roman was an "urban citizen." In the Germanic form, the individual was not a citizen. But whatever the precise form of landownership, wealth creation was not the aim of production among the ancients.[5]

Moderns have reversed the ancients. Among the ancients, humans were the object of production. Among the moderns, production and wealth itself are the aims of human activity. Stripping away what Marx calls "the narrow bourgeois form," wealth is useful for the full development of human control over the forces of nature, and one's own natural creativity as well. The act of wealth creation, in its best sense, is the process by which people become more human and fulfilled.

In an economy dominated by the bourgeoisie, workers are wholly alienated, sacrificed to ends not their own. "The childlike world of the ancient" is superior if we accept limited self-development. The problem of the modern world is that limited self-development leaves us unsatisfied. In bourgeois society where people appear to be self-satisfied, civilization is vulgar and mean.

In this chapter I explicate Marx's analysis of the cooperative social relationships within early societies and how they dissolved into exploitative ones, leading ultimately to the highest level of exploitation, in capitalism. In chapter 12 I explore the newer developments in economic anthropology that raise doubts as to the completeness of Marx's understanding of early societies.

The History of Alienated Labor

Marx provides theories of why ancient communal organized societies developed into exploitative societies. He then marshals some historical examples as cases in point.

Dynamic change intervenes in a variety of ways to upset the conditions of production, which continually repeat themselves in a static society. The presence of private or communal property does not necessarily mean that a bourgeois system will soon develop. The existence of slavery or serfdom does not by itself foreshadow exploitative relationships. In ancient times slaves captured in warfare were either killed or integrated into the community. Individuals were not slaveholders. A conquered and subjugated tribe becomes, like land, simply more property belonging to the tribe. In communities based on landed property and agriculture the individual is only the user of the land. Each person is at bottom property, a slave subordinated to the purposes of the community.[6] For this reason, the acquisition of slaves and serfs by means of conquest by itself does not change the nature of society.

Social change, with its capacity to revolutionize class relationships, may come from two sources: population growth and technological change. The growth of population on fixed allotments of land is an important cause of social change. Such an occurrence places pressure on land and results in wars of conquest. This, in consequence, leads to slavery, to more public land and to more aristocrats in control of the community.[7] Pressure on the community means the community has to change.

An improvement in agricultural productivity derived from new methods of production, new combinations of labor and capital, or a longer working day "changes not only the objective conditions — that is, transforming village into town, the wilderness into agricultural clearings, and so on — but the producers change with it, by the emergence of new qualities . . . forming new power and new conceptions, new modes of intercourse, new needs, and new speech."[8]

These changes are a necessary but not a sufficient condition to bring about the dissolution of a traditional society. Although changes in the objective conditions of production occur, free labor and land are not necessary consequences. Agricultural societies are stable, particularly in their Oriental form. Only when, as a consequence of fundamental changes, persons acquire private property and behave like proprietors of private property and give up their collective existence can conditions arise that allow property to be bought and sold. It is only where private production exists that an individual can lose his property. At that moment traditional social organization dissolves. Certainly in Oriental societies change of such magnitude would have to come from outside forces because individuals in those societies would never intentionally abandon their communal ties.

In bourgeois society, the chains binding the individual to society can be broken by dissolving communal property. Peasants are separated from the land, and lose their status as one of a group of owners, and become workers who earn wages. Thus, a second connection between individuals and society is dissolved.

Also artisans can become detached from the community. Their tools become capital in the hands of others. In guilds, workers had their tools passed down by inheritance. This assured their livelihood. A craftsman could survive before completing a task by living off savings obtained from previous earnings. Apprentices who were bound to masters were never in want. They shared their masters' food.

Dissolution of guilds left artisans with the status of slaves or serfs. Similarly, the development of capitalism does not result in an improved condition of production, but converts the worker into a wage laborer detached from a secure base as a member of society. Labor becomes the enemy of capital. As soon as the process of dissolution of primitive forms of property occurs, the potential for slavery or serfdom exists. Craft mastery may survive, but it survives as a caste system.

As dissolution of the ancient form of land ownership continues, those who lose ownership without gaining craft skills, such as the Roman plebes, become retainers of the propertied classes in subordinate roles to their lords and masters.

Relations between classes become so unequal that in times of stress, people actually sell themselves into slavery. Greek and Roman writers erred in their analysis of plebeians and freedmen. They were writing at the time of Augustine, when rich and poor constituted the only real classes of citizen. Persons in need, no matter how noble in origin, required patrons. Plebeians forced to abandon agriculture passed into the limited status of citizen. These so-called freedmen, seeking patrons in order to survive, had only their labor power to exchange. This historic process of dissolution of primitive forms of property proceeds not only among guildsmen but among persons bound to the soil. All so-called free men in a capitalist society essentially had nothing of their own but their labor power, which they no longer employed for themselves and were forced to use to produce exchangeable goods.

The process of dissolution by which a mass of individuals becomes a nation of potentially free wage earners does not presuppose the disappearance of the previous sources of income or of the property relationships of these individuals. Only their use has been altered. Freed laborers have now freed resources, raw materials, money, and tools available for hire, purchase, or sale in the market.[9]

The upshot of this dissolution is altered relationships in society. The condition of free laborers no longer bound to the soil has turned them into living capital to be used by others. Classical economists, considering the original transformation of capital into money, argued that capitalists needed to produce raw materials, tools, and food in quantities sufficient to enable the worker to live before the completion of production. For this the capitalist must have accumulated savings to advance to the worker. But the dependence of labor on financial advances from capitalists gives capitalists, according to Marx, "the eternal right . . . to the fruit of other men's labors." The capitalist then claims that "the eternal right" is derived from the simple and just laws of the exchange of equivalents.

35

Capitalists advance the free laborer the value of his subsistence. The sources of the money that make the transformation possible are income from interest and mercantile profits. The merchant and moneylender are capable of hiring free labor only if that labor is detached from its traditional sources of subsistence as a result of historical processes already described. For instance, if the guild system is working in its traditional form, money cannot purchase looms to put people to work. But if capitalists with money find free laborers, means of subsistence, materials, or other property not already in use, then they are available for sale.

The age of dissolution was the age in which monetary wealth developed. But monetary wealth alone is not enough to turn itself into capital. Many ancient societies from Rome to Byzantium had monetary wealth and commerce. The only result was the domination of countryside over city. When traditional societies dissolve, monetary wealth buys the living labor power of the free worker. Land, labor, and money capital already exist. What separates them out is a historic process, a process of the dissolution of traditionally organized societies. It is this that enables money to turn into capital. Money by itself does not create a market economy with free labor.

The History of Dissolution
in England

As Marx read English economic history, English landowners dismissed their retainers in order to create a free market in land and labor during the last century. The retainers had by right consumed a share of the surplus produce of the land. Farmers drove out small villagers. Labor power was thrown onto the labor market. Dispossessed serfs were free from the relation of "clientship, villeinage, or service, but also free from all goods and chattels, from every real and objective form of existence, *free from all property.*" These people could beg, become vagabonds, steal, or sell labor power. The means of subsistence formerly consumed by lords or retainers could never be bought for money. Money had neither created nor accumulated this subsistence. All that happened was that the means of subsistence were thrown into the exchange market. The same was true for physical capital, such as spinning wheels and looms. Spinners and weavers were separated from their wheels and looms. Marx describes the change this way: "*Capital unites the masses of hands and instruments which are already there* [in existence]. This and only this is what characterizes it. *It brings them together under its sway.* This is its *real accumulation.*"[10]

Marx believes that the factory system did not facilitate the accumulation of real capital goods. They already existed. Capitalism and the factory system simply collected workers independent up to this time, now devoid of their equipment, and placed them under the control of factory owners.

Other factors aided the dissolution of preexisting relations of production. The circulation of masses of commodities creates new needs and raises the exchange value of native products, raising prices and so on. Whereas prior accumulations of objective means of production, such as raw materials and instruments, were available to dispossessed workers, monetary wealth helps detach labor power from individuals capable of work and places it under capitalist control.

It is not monetary wealth itself, gained by usury, trade, and hoarding by tenant farmers, that accounts for the bourgeois economy. It is production for the purpose of exchange, rather than use, that brings about the dissolution of labor's former relation to land.

Money, however, is easily transformed into capital. Taking spinners and weavers out of cottage industry, where they were subsidiary occupations, and putting them into factories, where they are dependent on the buyer and the merchant, producing solely for him and by means of him as supplier of raw material, they produce exchange values. In purchasing their labor the merchant first takes away the worker's property in product, then takes away the instrument of production.[11]

Marx's Conclusion

"We thus see," Marx writes, "that the transformation of money into capital presupposes a historic process which separates the objective conditions of labor, and makes them independent of and sets them against the laborers. However, once capital and its process have come into being, they conquer all production and everywhere bring about and accentuate the separation between labor and property, labor and the objective conditions of labor. . . . [We can also see] in what ways capital destroys artisan labor, small working land ownership . . . and all other old modes of production. . . . The only accumulation [necessary for the use of capital] is monetary wealth, which [by itself is] unproductive. [Money] emerges from circulation to create internal markets, destroying all rural subsidiary crafts."[12] Use values are turned into exchange values, separating labor from the soil and property, turning the product of human labor into a commodity.

The major outcome of this process is the production of capitalists and laborers. Capital is the capitalist. Also, production is capital; money is capital. Capital is loaned; capital is accumulated. The product of living labor is converted from an abstraction to a real thing and in the process of converting traditional economies into bourgeois economies is turned into an abstract thing.

Summary

Small landowning is not exploitative or alienating. Individuals may own private land and use land in common without destroying the use value of land. The dissolution of communal bonds comes gradually over history as people are slowly separated from the means of production. Land becomes alienated, and tools, in the hands of others than the artisan, become capital.

The breakdown of traditional society was slow. Social change came from outside (as with an invasion), or from within (because of increased population), or through productivity (which upsets stable relationships). The development of monetary wealth in circulation does not cause "dissolution" by itself. But if (as in a city) there are free laborers and materials of production available, money can be gathered together as capital and labor. Enter the capitalist, who exploits the alienated relationship of individuals and their land and equipment.

From such observations Marx argues that the social consequences of alienation are deeply embedded in the realities of the economy. Worker and owner even in precapitalist societies are locked in a fatal embrace, an embrace not of their own choosing, but one created for them by the dynamic of the social reality of which they are a part.

Marx belongs to the school of "substantivists," for whom market domination of society is a historically new and socially unstable situation. Alienation is its consequence and results in continuous protest throughout the nineteenth century. For Karl Polanyi, author of *The Great Transformation,* no less a catastrophe than World War I can be traced to the "utopian" idea that society can be run as an adjunct of the market.

"Formalists," by contrast, discover all motivations of market societies hidden in what appear to be ceremonial and highly constrained modes of exchange found throughout history in preindustrial societies. People everywhere and under all historical circumstances behave "economically." They optimize the output of valued commodities and minimize input costs. Formalists believe Marx undervalued exchange as a means of improving human well-being and point out that all parties can gain from exchange on markets. Marx, they believe, overemphasized the exploitative characteristic of markets. They challenge his claim that cities always exploit the countryside. Formalists find evidence for the existence of prices, profits, and production in response to market signals. Marx, from the formalist point of view, overemphasizes the distinction between the modern and premodern worlds and to that extent exaggerates the growth of alienation.

There is a more eclectic view melding both schools. Although markets appear to have been ubiquitous in precapitalist societies, systems of exchange seem to vary widely depending upon cultural differences. The modes of production do not seem to have set the agenda in all previous societies. The eclectic view holds that cultural and political elements may set the terms upon which exchange occurs. Thus, at the same time that they deny the universal primacy of economic factors in human history, they challenge Marx's central conclusion that market orientation of society is a new phenomenon coincident with the industrial revolution.

In chapter 5 we look at competing analyses of the evil consequences of industrial capitalism enunciated by critics during the nineteenth century. For Marx to promulgate the Marxist System persuasively, he had first to investigate the theories and programs of other social critics of his day and demonstrate their irrelevance to real improvement in the condition of the working class. The critics he challenged may be divided into three categories: reformers, non-Marxist socialists, and anarchists.

CHAPTER 5

SCIENTIFIC SOCIALISM, SOCIALISM, AND ANARCHISM

Marx and Engels believed that their understanding of the processes by which the world operated was supported by the authority of the natural sciences. If the physical world ran on knowable principles, the social world did so as well. Just as one discovered laws of change and evolution in the world of nature, so the world of interacting humans could be knowable.

On these grounds Marx and Engels developed the Marxist System, which ascribed the failure of other would-be leaders to their lack of understanding of the principles of "scientific socialism." Without recourse to scientific authority, they misperceived the problems facing workers and thus recommended solutions that could not but fail.

Important to the Marxist System was the understanding of "history" as moving forward under its own momentum. Humans would in the long run achieve the high destiny they deserved. Nevertheless, leadership well trained in scientific socialism was necessary to escort society to that destination. Marx bitterly and sarcastically attacked the extant forms of socialism, referring to them as "feudal," "petty bourgeois," and "German" or as "true," "conservative" or "bourgeois," and finally, as "utopian."

There had developed in nineteenth-century Europe a mutant form of socialism, which Marx saw as dangerous because of its attraction to the naive masses, and with which he was in perpetual battle: anarchism. Anarchism at its heart advocated a society without government, spontaneously controlled by the interaction of autonomous groups. It was among the useless and foolish programs of socialist and near-socialist heretics that Marx expected would be abandoned once social leaders came to understand the scientific basis of his own system. Indeed, all other leaders would necessarily become Marxists and accept the primacy of Marx as guru of the working class. Marx, in the meantime, spent most of his life fighting those he saw as well-meaning but essentially ignorant socialists, anarchists, and bourgeois reformers who flourished during his own lifetime without the benefit of his insight.

This chapter deals with Marx's criticism of some of the major nonscientific socialist and anarchist programs of his day, all of which were advocated by radicals and reformers who had in common their condemnation of the callousness of the emerging industrial system and its heartless bourgeois leadership. They also had in common, according to Marx, a fatal misunderstanding of the true nature of the problem facing the working class.

Marx on Other Socialisms

The *Communist Manifesto* and *Socialism, Scientific and Utopian* discuss alternative socialisms. One alternative form of socialism is feudal socialism, which Marx and Engels see as reactionary. Aristocrats, to arouse sympathy for the restoration of their own power, cynically attack their "new masters," the bourgeoisie, in the name of the exploited proletariat. Their attack was ridiculous in its effect, through its total incapacity to comprehend the march of modern history. English landlords, for example, first enlisted the "parsons" to attack the rising industrialists. Clerical socialism and feudal socialism joined forces, a phenomenon Marx views with a ridicule and an irony that have no bounds. "Has not Christianity declaimed against private property, against marriage, against the State? [and in favor of] charity and poverty, celibacy and mortification of the flesh, monastic life and Mother Church? Christian Socialism is but holy water with which the priest consecrates the heart-burnings of the aristocrat."[1]

The petty bourgeoisie (artisans, small peasant proprietors, townsfolk typical of the medieval town) were also "ruined" by the bourgeoisie. The advent of competitive capitalism always threatened to hurl them down into the ranks of the proletariat. The aim of the petty bourgeoisie was to undo the industrial revolution, its division of labor, disastrous effects of machinery, the concentration of capital, overproduction, inequality of wealth, misery of the proletariat, ruin of peasant agriculture, and finally the destruction of old moral bonds and family relations. Again, the responses of landlords and parsons were reactionary. The time had passed when corporate guilds and patriarchal relations in agriculture could be restored. An idyllic stability in economic, social, and religious life was forever beyond retrieval.[2]

German or "true" socialism was the result of the infusion of French revolutionary ideals into German idealism. French revolutionary ideas incorporated the much older French idea that there existed in the French nation a "General

Will," which in eighteenth-century France could be translated as the will of the rising bourgeoisie. In the Germany of the eighteenth century there was not yet a bourgeoisie whose will was evident. The German philosophers therefore converted the French General Will into the Will of all humans, thereby stripping it of all power of action. "True" socialism thereby became a "literary" movement, one that discussed such abstract concepts as the "Philosophy of Action," "German Science and Socialism," and "Philosophic Foundations of Socialism." German socialists, without a proletariat, lacked revolutionary content and could be adopted by absolutist feudal governments "with their following of parsons, professors, country squires. . . . [serving] as a welcome scarecrow against the threatening bourgeoisie."[3] "True" socialism served reactionary interests.

Socialism: Scientific and Utopian

Modern socialism, as explained by Marx and Engels, originated with the great French philosophers of the eighteenth century. For those revolutionaries, everything was subject to criticism. No institution was spared, no traditional idea was held sacred. To these philosophers "the kingdom of reason" would banish all superstition, privilege, and oppression. "Eternal truth, eternal right, and equality based on Nature and the inalienable rights of man"[4] would triumph.

On closer examination, Marx and Engels found the French philosophers' kingdom of reason was nothing more than the "idealized kingdom of the bourgeoisie",[5] the right to justice was to bourgeois justice, and the rights before the law were the ultimate rights of property. Rousseau's social contract could come into being only in a bourgeois republic, the bourgeoisie presenting themselves as champions not of one special class but of all suffering humanity. The "rights of man" were the property rights of the growing middle class, certainly not the rights of workers, let alone all humankind. The French socialists were really reformers concerned with establishing bourgeois democracy, not the emancipation of human beings.

The bourgeoisie trumpeted the rights of "man" because capitalists cannot exist without wage workers: the journeyman, the day laborer—in short, the proletariat. In their struggle with the nobility, the French philosophers could argue that they were struggling for everyone, but in Engels's mind they could not really represent anyone but themselves.

Out of the middle class came three great utopians: the Comte Henri de Saint-Simon, François Fourier, and Robert Owen, all children of the Enlightenment, all rationalists. Interestingly, none of the three appears to have represented the interests of the proletariat. They saw their task as the enlightenment of humankind. Reason was to be the supreme arbiter.

Engels saw danger in depending on reason for social justice. He argued that the French Revolution, which believed itself predicated on rational government and rational society of the type advocated by the French philosophers, created a state that collapsed completely. The logic of Rousseau's social contract resulted in France in the Reign of Terror, the Directorate, and in the despot Napoleon. All institutions that protected the poor and the working class were wiped away in the general rush to rid French society of its protective feudal forms. As Engels saw it, endless war and hideous poverty were the legacies of the rule of reason. The removal of "feudal fetters" resulted in unfettered capitalism. And with capitalism came corruption, cheating, and chicanery. The *droit de seigneur* was transferred from feudal lords to bourgeois manufacturers. The serf, peasant, and artisan were turned into wage slaves without rights or protection. In short, Engels disposes of the utopian claims of the eighteenth-century rationalists and minimizes the achievements of the French Revolution. Such, he says, is the havoc wrought by well-meaning utopians whose thoughts arise not from scientific examination of a historical experience but derive from reason.

Engels goes on to analyze the three utopians—Saint-Simon, Fourier, and Owen. All held that the conflict they saw could be alleviated by change in the industrial order. They also tried to solve social problems intellectually. Not understanding the science of history, let alone scientific socialism, they failed to realize that the world had not evolved sufficiently for them to see the issues clearly or to perceive that the time was not yet ripe for the solutions that they advocated.

The first utopian discussed by Engels is Saint-Simon. Saint-Simon thought the conflict lay between idlers and workers. Idlers were the old privileged class and people who lived off their incomes. Workers were not only wage workers but manufacturers, bankers, and merchants. Thus, science and industry united in a "new Christianity," which was "necessarily mystic and rigidly hierarchic." Bankers were to lead social production; the bourgeoisie were to be "social trustees," public officials, holding a commanding position with respect to workers. Saint-Simon, looking at a world he saw as corrupt and degrading, challenged the bourgeoisie who spouted about progress, freedom, and universal happiness to reorganize society so as to achieve the reality behind their high-sounding phrases.[6]

Engels purports to admire Saint-Simon because he is the first to hold that all men have a right to work and that the French Revolution was a class war not simply between nobility and bourgeoisie but between them both and non-possessors. He foresaw the absorption of politics by economics, understanding that economic conditions are the basis of political institutions. Finally, he looked to the "abolition of the state" when political rule over society would be replaced by "the administration of things," all developments that Engels and Marx also foresaw. Saint-Simon was to be admired for the enormous breadth of his thought; however, change would never come by persuading capitalists of this vision.

Next, Engels turned to Fourier. To Engels, Fourier is great not only as a critic, but also as a satirist. He depicts with "equal power and charm" the swindling speculator who blossomed with the downfall of the revolution and the shopkeeping mentality prevalent during the revolution. Also he is the first to measure the emancipation of society by the degree of emancipation of women.[7]

Engels reserves his greatest praise of Fourier for his conception of history, which the utopian sees as divided "into four stages of evolution—savagery, barbarism, the patriarchate, [and] civilization."[8] The last is today's bourgeois society. Modern civilization "raises every vice [of] barbarism . . . into a form of existence, complex, ambiguous, equivocal, hypocritical."[9] Civilization moves in vicious circles without being able to solve contradictions. It arrives at the opposite of what it wants. "Poverty is born of super-abundance itself."

Fourier uses the dialectical method as masterfully as does Hegel. But unlike Hegel, who foresees an arrival at the heights of human perfection, Fourier presages the ultimate destruction of the human race. In the France of Fourier, "the sluggish march of development of the manufacturing period changed into a veritable storm and stress period of production."[10] The splitting-up of society into capitalists and nonpossessing proletariat grew on, leaving those in between — artisans, small shopkeepers, the formerly stable middle class—in a precarious position. For this insight too, Engels admired Fourier.

Finally, Engels considers England's Robert Owen a reformer, a manufacturer, "a man of almost sublime, childlike simplicity of character"—yet a born leader. Owen saw only confusion and the opportunity to fish in the troubled waters of industrialization, thus making a large fortune. Putting into operation his own theory of how to bring order out of chaos, from 1800 to 1829 Owen managed the great cotton mills at New Lanark in Scotland. Confronted with a diverse population that grew to 2500, he constructed a model colony without "drunkenness, public magistrates, lawsuits, poor laws and charity." Owen accomplished this feat, according to Engels, by placing "people in conditions worthy of human beings." Owen was especially concerned with the future generation. He built infant schools where children enjoyed themselves, cut the workday to 10.5 hours from the prevailing 13 to 14, and paid people when they were laid off during the downturns in the business cycle.

Although Robert Owen made vast amounts of money, he recognized the shortcomings of his program. "The people were slaves at my mercy."[11] He admitted he had not improved their intellect and character. More important, he saw that the huge profits he made for his stockholders had been earned by the Napoleonic wars and acknowledged that he had enslaved the masses to enrich the few.

At this point, in 1823, Owen secured his own downfall. He proposed communist societies in Ireland, recommending that workers own their factories. Engels remarks that so long as Owen was a philanthropist, he "was rewarded with nothing but wealth, applause, honors and glory." But when he espoused communist themes, the statesmen and princes who had listened to him turned away. He soon saw that private property, religion, and marriage blocked him. He knew that if he attacked these institutions, "outlawry, excommunication from official society, the loss of his whole social position" were sure to follow.[12]

And evil did befall this well-intentioned man: He lost a fortune in communist experiments in America; the press and official society banished him from society by a conspiracy of silence. On the other hand, he pressed successfully for passage of the first law limiting the hours of work of women and children in factories. He anticipated Proudhon's bank of exchange long before its time. And he began cooperative societies which eventually evolved into the British labor movement. In short, he did much to reform social ills as he saw them.

Engels's own analysis of utopian socialists was that they were doomed to failure because "[to] all these socialism is the expression of absolute truth, reason and justice, and has only to be discovered to conquer all the world by virtue of its own power. . . . They saw truth, reason and justice as absolute truth independent of time, space and the historical development of man."[13]

Socialism and Anarchism

Marx saw anarchism as a far more formidable foe than other forms of socialism, which he believed to be impotent. Engels stated the case against anarchism succinctly. At the time of Marx's death in 1883, he wrote, "Marx and I . . . have held the view that one of the final results of the future proletarian revolution will be the gradual dissolution and ultimate disappearance of that political organization called *the State*; an organization the main object of which has ever been to secure, by armed force, the economical subjection of the working majority to the wealthy minority. With the disappearance of a wealthy minority the necessity for an armed repressive State-force disappears also. At the same time we have always held that in order to arrive at this and the other, far more important ends of the social revolution of the future, the proletarian class will first have to possess itself of the organized political force of the State and with this aid stamp out the resistance of the Capitalist class and re-organize society. . . .

"The Anarchists reverse the matter. They say that the Proletarian revolution has to *begin* by abolishing the political organization of the State. But after the victory of the Proletariat, the only organization the victorious working class finds ready-made for use is that of the State. It may require adaptation to the new functions. But to destroy that at such a moment, would be to destroy the only organism by means of which the victorious working class can exert its newly conquered power, keep down its capitalist enemies and carry out that economic revolution of society without which the whole victory must end in a defeat and in a massacre of the working class like that after the Paris Commune. . . ."[14]

Marx's lifelong battle against anarchist doctrine began at the time of his break with the companions of his youth, the Young Hegelians (see chapter 12). In 1845, Max Stirner (1806-56) published an attack on Ludwig Feuerbach's *Essence of Christianity* in his book entitled *The Individual and His Own*. Stirner's central concern was domination. He accuses Feuerbach of oppressive spirituality despite Feuerbach's claim to have neutralized spirituality. Isaiah Berlin's summary of Stirner's position helps explain his attack on Feuerbach and on Marx as well. Berlin writes: "Stirner believed that all programmes, ideals, theories, are so many artificially built prisons for the mind and the spirit, means of curbing the will, of concealing from the individual the existence of his own infinite creative powers, and that all systems must therefore be destroyed, not because they are evil, but because they are systems; only when this has been achieved, would man, released from his unnatural fetters, become truly master of himself and attain to his full stature as a human being."[15] To claim that humans need spirituality was to claim that humans need a religious dominance.

Marx, in *The German Ideology*, excoriates and ridicules Stirner. The idea that individuals, each inherently different from the other, can exist outside a social context is, to Marx, absurd. Marx himself finds the variety of talents found in people to be a consequence of the capitalist environment in which they live, particularly the division of labor. For Marx, as we see in chapter 13, persons have the inherent capability to become whatever they wish to be.

Stirner appeared to be in favor of rebellion and against revolution. Revolution requires organization and a program, to which Stirner objects because it involves the sacrifice of the individual to another form of dominance. Rebellion was to take place spontaneously and without planned goals. Marx, not surprisingly, found the distinction between rebellion and revolution incoherent.

Pierre Proudhon (1809–65) was an anarchist with whom Marx was engaged in mortal combat (see chapter 13). If Stirner drove his conception of the free-floating individual in isolation to its absurd but logical conclusion, Proudhon did not. His anarchism was limited to an abhorrence of government, any government. He wrote: "To be *governed* is to be kept under surveillance, inspected, spied upon, bossed, law-ridden, regulated, penned-in, indoctrinated, preached at, registered, evaluated, appraised, censured, ordered about by creatures who have neither the right, nor the knowledge, nor the virtue, to do so. . . . It is, under the pretence of public benefit and in the name of the general interest, to be requisitioned, drilled, fleeced, exploited, monopolized, extorted, squeezed, hoaxed, robbed; then at the slightest resistance, the first word of complaint, to be squelched, corrected, vilified, bullied, hounded, tormented, bludgeoned, disarmed, strangled, imprisoned, shot down, judged, condemned, deported, sacrificed, sold, betrayed, and to top it off, ridiculed, made a fool of, outraged, dishonored. That's government, that's justice, that's morality!"[16]

Proudhon's hostility to government might have been music to Marx's ears had Proudhon's attitude extended to capitalist governments alone. But Proudhon's hatred of all government Marx believed to be dangerous. When Marx read Proudhon's book *What Is Property?* (1840), the famous answer to which was "Property Is Theft," Marx was full of praise for its forthright courage. But when *The Philosophy of Poverty* (1846) appeared, Marx decided that its message and the reputation of its author must be destroyed. In Marx's reply, *The Misery of Philosophy,* he accused Proudhon of falsely interpreting the Hegelian dialectic to refer to the struggle between good and evil, a position that reflected Proudhon's own strong moral convictions. Marx declared that Proudhon understood neither Hegel's philosophy nor Ricardo's economics. For Hegel, according to Marx, progress required that *both* sides of a dialectic argument be ultimately destroyed. Good against evil was hardly the issue. Marx argued that whereas Proudhon believed that labor time *should* determine the value of a commodity, Ricardo held that it *did*.

Of Proudhon's stance, it was radical individualism, however, that challenged Marx and scientific socialism most. Proudhon's individual, unlike Stirner's, was not an abstract timeless and placeless being. According to Proudhon, there already existed yeoman farmers in France who were sturdy and moral men. To be free they required some private farm property. For stability there needed to be a strong (male-dominated) family life.

To Marx his policies seemed eccentric. He opposed revolutionary activity and violence, advocated political abstention on the part of working people, and opposed trade union activity that might lead to strikes. He proposed a program typical of anarchism, a decentralized federation of political units, which, as part of the program of the Paris Commune, Marx later appeared to support (see chapter 14). Workers as individuals were to organize institutions spontaneously and voluntarily. He advocated societies for the provision of funds for mutual aid, and workers' credit.

The anarchist most troublesome to Marx was Mikhail Bakunin (1814-76). His disagreements with Bakunin were much like those with Proudhon—political and ideological. The struggle for personal power that obsessed both Marx and Bakunin as well as diametrically opposite conceptions of liberation strategy led ultimately to Bakunin's expulsion from the International and the dissolution of that organization (see chapter 14). Bakunin, a well-born Russian, hated czarism, all injustice, gradualism as strategy for reform, and all impediments to individual freedom.

Like Proudhon but unlike Stirner, Bakunin believed in organization. Whereas Proudhon believed in orderly, nonviolent worker control of workplaces, Bakunin believed in secret, conspiratorial working-men's cells, widely decentralized and not averse to violence. He purported to oppose political movements while supporting economic goals. He encouraged factory-by-factory agitation for the eight-hour working day and encouraged use of the strike weapon. Marx was moved to comment that Bakunin did not understand that the sum of individual economic agitation everywhere became de facto political activity.

Marx derided Bakunin's program for the ultimately triumphant working class once it had disposed of capitalism. That program consisted of four elements—slogans, it would appear, because the elements contained no substance. They were (1) achieving equality of classes, (2) abolishing inheritance, (3) declaring atheism official dogma for members of conspiratorial cells (which were to be maintained after government was abolished), and (4) abstaining from politics. Marx remarked once that though a nonentity as a theoretician, Bakunin was in his element as an intriguer.

Most interesting for us is the similarity of Bakunin's secret cells to Lenin's "front" organizations as the vanguard of revolution. Both stand in contrast to the rather open workers' organizations favored by Marx. Marx and Lenin saw intellectuals serving as tutors to the working class. Bakunin's cells were independent of mass worker organizations, and revolutionary programs were believed to be capable of being carried forward by small unattached groups working alone. Lenin, who never believed that small revolutionary groups could win without mass support, had a dual organizational structure. On the one hand there was to be a large number of small groups of professional revolutionaries; on the other hand, proletarian masses. When political and economic conditions were right, the masses would follow the leadership. Meanwhile, the masses must be continuously educated. The cadres of militant and dedicated revolutionaries would continue to exist when, as frequently happened, the masses deserted the leadership.

Summary

Marx holds that socialists (other than scientific socialists) and anarchists fall into the error of failing to understand the complexity of human processes, particularly the dialectic process. That process is evolutionary and carries change within itself. It is no good for intelligent, well-meaning men like Saint-Simon, Fourier, Owen, Proudhon, Stirner, and Bakunin to "think up" rational ideas for other men of goodwill to implement or to imagine ideal states that may be achieved by agitation or force. Ideas become realities in their time and place. They appear reasonable when society is historically ready for them. The conditions that bring about social change are complex and interrelated. Change occurs according to scientifically correct dialectical processes. The socialism that is scientific springs, in its proper time, from the web of social facts and conditions whose meaning lies hidden beneath the boiling and bubbling surface of the world. Socialism will ultimately arrive because the science of dialectical change proves it to be so. Socialism arrives in the natural order of things. Dialectical theory so dictates.

Meanwhile, after Marx's death in 1883, all varieties of socialism blossomed in a number of shapes and forms. Each European country followed its own radical traditions, perhaps tinged with the language of Marx, but essentially heretical. Each socialist party responded to the sociopolitical conditions in which it was embedded.

In Germany, home of Marx's most numerous adherents, Marxism was revised. Eduard Bernstein (1850–1932), a friend and literary executor of Engels and an orthodox Marxist, philosopher, and political activist, brought the Social Democratic party into the mainstream of German politics. He abandoned Hegelian dialectics along with Marx's apocalyptic vision of the death of capitalism. There was no political future for a political party that talked revolution while the living standards of workers were rising or of the international brotherhood of workers while German nationalism was still ascendant. And although participation in Bismarck's parliament conferred no real power, the ballot box held more promise than force.

In France, radical political parties were in shreds. There were French socialists as well as remnants of the radical and revolutionary movements descended from the anarchism of Proudhon and Bakunin and the violent and conspiratorial Jacobins and Blanquists. Although French socialists had access to political power as early as 1899 and could have taken the path of the Social Democrats in Germany, the real force in French politics were the trade unions, the *syndicat*. Syndicalism pursued the class struggle by means of a strategy that would destroy capitalism and the state. Trade unions were to take control of factories by whatever means necessary—strikes, boycotts, sabotage, violence, and intimidation—and, if possible, create anarchy by means of general strikes. Revolution not economic improvement, anarchy not democracy, was their aim.

Though claiming to be heirs of Marx, French socialists were romantic revolutionaries of the kind that Marx abhorred. Their goal was a voluntaristic society like that advocated by anarchists but different in that the center of social activity would be trade unions rather than local communities. Syndicalists were philosophically closer to fascism than to socialism, as Engels saw the matter.

In France as in Germany, democratic socialism gradually triumphed over syndicalism. In Russia, however, repression of all dissent by the czars created a revolutionary underground. Unbelievable mismanagement of Russian forces during World War I led to enormous casualties. War weariness provided the opportunity for revolution.

V.I. Lenin (1870-1924), a revolutionary and theoretician, set out to bring Marxism to Russia. Marx, it will be remembered, refused to provide more than an outline of a future communist society. He also expected socialism to fall heir to the capitalist engine of production. Lenin had the will and power to redefine Marxism to suit the conditions of a country whose industrial revolution lagged behind that of Western Europe. Russia, in the late nineteenth century, was largely a society of peasants and in virtual chaos.

Lenin is credited with bringing Marxism to Russia and establishing the first socialist state. Socialism in conditions of underdevelopment required a shift of emphasis from wealth redistribution to that of wealth creation. And the process of forced industrialization under the ungentle hand of Joseph Stalin (1879-1953) defined socialism until our time. Whereas Marxism was concerned with social justice, to some extent a matter of income distribution, the Soviet variety of Marxism concentrated on economic growth.

In England, where Marxism never flourished as a popular creed, a wide variety of socialist doctrines, going all the way back to Robert Owen, continued their emphasis on social justice and democratic reform. The British welfare state created after World War II, the remnants of which are the health services, was the fruit of socialism's long history.

As a generalization, those Marxists who held firmly to socialism as social justice remained faithful to democratic traditions and goals. Those descendants of Marx who headed directly for socialism in countries without democratic traditions and an industrial base created so-called Marxist States and their attendant cultures.

Chapter 6 is concerned with the materialist conception of history, which is the cornerstone of the Marxist System, and elucidates Marx's analysis of how history actually works itself out over time.

THE MATERIALIST CONCEPTION OF HISTORY

The running dispute of Marx and Engels with most of their contemporary social critics was not about their common goal of an emancipated, freely functioning and creative life for members of the human race. All contenders were optimists who believed that the future held a bright promise if only society could be reformed. They agreed on goals.

But Marx did not agree with the "utopian" socialists who believed that rational argument would persuade powerful people to use their property in the interest of social good or that, in the consequently supportive surroundings, common people would reform their evil ways. Marx looked to the materialist conception of history to explain how a civilization and its people change.

To make people free Marx and Engels counted not on rational argument but on underlying social forces that would provide incentives for people to do right. They held to a curious double view of the social process. They accepted the Enlightenment belief in the ultimate triumph of progress for the human race. In *The German Ideology* Marx says that "History" in due course will bring improvement. On the other hand humans have to work at making things come out right. "Men make their own history, but do not make it just as they please, nor out of conditions which they choose themselves. They must take the world as they find it, working with materials close at hand."

One strand in Marxism argues that history has its own agenda, another that change occurs only through the agency of people. Marx believes that the problem with "utopian" and other socialists is that they vastly underrate the importance of the existence of a proper social structure—the historical condition—for effective action. The materialist conception of history explains the importance of history being "ready" for human actors to take control of their fate.

"The premises from which we begin are not arbitrary ones, not dogmas, but real premises from which abstraction can only be made in the imagination."[1] The premises are real people who live under real material conditions and "these premises can be verified in a purely empirical way"[2] when they are examined. In *Preface to Political Economy* Marx declares: "At a certain stage of their development, the material productive forces of society come in conflict with the existing relations of production, or—what is but a legal expression for the same thing—with the property relations within which they have been at work hitherto. From forms of development of the productive forces these relations turn into their fetters. Then begins an epoch of social revolution."[3]

Starting from the first premise of all human history, which is the existence of living human individuals, the first fact to be established is the physical organization of those individuals and their consequent relation to the rest of the natural world. The individual lives in a "natural setting with its own particular characteristics, geological, hydrographical, climatic and so forth."[4]

Men are distinguished from animals by consciousness, religion, and especially by their ability to produce their means of subsistence. By producing their means of subsistence they are indirectly producing their actual material life.

The way men in fact produce their subsistence depends on the natural means at their disposal. They do not simply reproduce their physical existence, but create forms that express their lives. What they are coincides with what they produce and how they produce. The nature of persons thus depends on the material conditions that determine their production.[5]

Nations differ from one another in the extent to which each develops productive forces, the division of labor, and social systems. The whole internal structure of a nation depends on its stage of development of production and its internal and external intercourse. Each new productive force adds to the division of labor.

The internal division of labor leads to a separation of industry and commerce from agricultural labor. The division between town and country leads to a clash of interests between them. As the division of labor develops, branches of labor develop; the relative division of labor determines the social position of persons. Methods employed by agriculture, industry, and commerce proliferate. There are just as many modes of ownership as there are existing stages of division of labor.

Marx's anthropology, found in part in *The German Ideology*, clearly shows the relationship among tools (available technology), the property system, civilization and the course of history. Marx describes the evolution of bourgeois society this way: The first form of ownership is tribal; people live by hunting and fishing, and by rearing beast. Later they undertake agricultural activity.

The division of labor is still elementary, and the natural distribution of labor is imposed on a family. The social structure is limited to the extension of the family. As part of the family there may be patriarchal chieftains. Below them are members of the tribe, and finally, the slaves. Slavery develops later, with population growth, the growth of wants, and the extension of external relations for war or for trade.

The second form of ownership, which proceeds directly from the union of several tribes into a city by agreement or conquest, includes the ancient commune and state ownership, still accompanied by slavery. Movable and immovable private properties develop, but as an abnormal form, subordinate to communal ownership. The community as a whole, not as individuals, owns slaves.

In chapter 4, it was shown that in ancient societies alienation and exploitation did not occur. This chapter explains the origin of these evils by insisting that in cities the entire structure of communal private property decays to the same degree that immovable private property evolves. In the process the division of labor, already well developed in preurban societies, results in conflicts of interest between town and country. Inside the towns themselves antagonism between industry and maritime commerce emerges. The class relation between citizens and slaves becomes completely developed.

The third form of ownership is feudal, or estate, property. The Middle Ages started with the rise of the countryside and the decline of cities. Population densities determine starting points. As the Roman Empire declined through the destruction of productive forces, agriculture, industry, and trade were suspended. The urban population decreased. Out of these conditions feudalism developed, influenced by Germanic militarism. No slavery accompanied this new condition, but the producing class stood against the enserfed small peasantry. With feudalism fully developed, antagonism arose between town and country. The nobility, by the use of armed retainers, held sway over the serfs. Again, in feudalism the issue was an association of ruling classes against producing classes. The form of that association differed in accordance with different conditions of production.

The feudal organization of land had its counterparts in towns in the form of corporate property. Property consisted of the labor of each individual. Associations of artisans were formed into guilds organized against "robber nobility" and competing industrial merchants.

Escaped serfs swarmed into rising towns, threatening the feudal structure of the entire country. Further, the accumulated capital of individual craftsmen and their stable numbers protected them against a rising population of journeymen and apprentices, so that hierarchies developed in the town that were similar to those in the country.

The chief forms of property in feudal times consisted of landed property and serf labor chained to it in the country; individual laborers with small capital commanded journeymen in the towns. Organizations of both were determined by the conditions of production. There was little division of labor in the heyday of feudalism.

Larger groupings into feudal kingdoms were as necessary for the nobility as for towns. A ruling class was needed, with a monarch at its head. "The fact is that individuals who are productively active in a definite way enter into definite social and political relations. Observation of the historical record proves beyond doubt the connection of the social and political structures."[6] The state and social structure are continually evolving out of real-life processes of individuals as they really are, limited in their activities by the social and physical conditions under which they live.[7]

Ideas, conceptions, and the like are at first interwoven with material activity, the material of intercourse, "the language of real life." Humans are the producers of their conceptions, ideas; they are conditioned by their economic environment. Human understanding of the world comes from their experience in it, although people's understanding of the world may not reflect its reality.[8]

The Material Base of Human History

The strand of Marxist thought that postulates that history, the passage of time itself, brings progress is illustrated by the relationship between the ever-improving modes of production, mainly technological, and the changing nature of society.

In *The German Ideology* Marx comments that real history cannot be understood unless its material base is understood. Thus the German romantic speculative philosophers, who failed to ground their thought in materialism, could never understand historical processes.[9]

Marx does not deny that human progress will take place even without humans understanding what is really occurring. Yet the strand of thought most commonly associated with Marx and the stance taken in the *Communist Manifesto* argue that social change is a consequence of class struggle, that the outcome of this struggle is not foreordained and depends on how well the structure of power in society is understood. Human activity must be intelligent as well as purposeful. Marxism based on materialism provides the tools; humans need to control history.

In *The Communist Manifesto*, written much earlier than *The German Ideology*, Marx and Engels deal with the transformation of society from feudal to capitalist. They argue that the underlying economic conditions resulting in the dissolution of the medieval world created the two great classes—the bourgeoisie and proletariat—that were presently engaged in a titanic struggle. As with the struggle between the landed aristocracy and the bourgeoisie, the issue between the proletariat and the bourgeoisie was over economic interests that political power was to serve. Bourgeoisie and proletariat both arose from the transformation of economic conditions. The transition, first from guild handicraft to manufacturing, then to large-scale industry, steam and mechanical power, had caused the development of the two great classes.

Engels describes his and Marx's position clearly in *Ludwig Feuerbach*: "At a certain stage the new productive forces set in motion by the bourgeoisie . . . became incompatible with the existing order of production handed down by history and sanctified by law."[10]

Productive techniques came to be incompatible with the privileges of the guild and the numerous other privileges of a stratified feudal order of society. The productive forces represented by the bourgeoisie rebelled against the order of production represented by feudal landlords and guild masters. The results are known. "The feudal fetters were smashed, gradually in England [and] at one blow in France. In Germany the process is not yet finished."[11]

Today large-scale industry has come into conflict with the "bourgeois order of production." Capitalism at this stage is unable to contain the contradiction of enormous capitalist production on the one hand and the "ever-increasing proletarianization of the great mass of the people on the other." Overproduction of salable goods and mass misery cause each other, the absurd outcome of capitalism. The contradiction of misery in the presence of plenty "calls for the liberation of the productive forces by means of a change in the mode of production," a change in the economic system.[12]

In modern history, "all political struggles are class struggles, and all class struggles for emancipation, despite their necessarily political form . . . turn ultimately on the question of economic emancipation."[13] The state is subordinate to civil society. Economic relationships are decisive. Hegel saw the state as the determining element, and economic elements as responding to it. But these were just "appearances." "As all the driving forces of the actions of any individual persons must pass through his brain, and transform themselves into motives of his will in order to set him into action, so all the needs of civil society (economic society)—no matter which class happens to be the ruling one—must pass through the will of the state in order to secure general validity in the form of laws."[14]

If we enquire as to why the will of the ruling classes and not another dominates, the answer is "that in modern history the will of the state is, on the whole, determined by the changing needs of civil society, by the supremacy of this or that class, in the last resort, by the development of the productive forces and relations of exchange."[15]

If the state and public laws are determined by economic relations, so too is private law, which must sanction the relations of individuals. In some instances, as in England, the forces of economic relations that existed in feudal times were "in harmony" with the whole of national development. All that was necessary to bring feudal law into harmony with new economic relationships was to give them bourgeois content.

In Western Europe, Roman law, "the first world law of commodity-producing society," could be used as the foundation of law, adjusted by judicial practice (as in common law) or, it could "with the help of allegedly enlightened moralizing jurists" become consistent with economic conditions, as circumstances required.

Marx and Engels, in *Feuerbach* and earlier in the *Manifesto*, compared the struggle between the landed aristocracy and the emergent bourgeoisie for economic power with the newer struggle between the bourgeoisie and the proletariat. Both were caused by the impact of changes in technology on social relationships. But the earlier conflict between two ruling classes is now replaced by tensions between the new ruling class and its victims, the workers.

Further Explanations of the Materialist Conception

After Marx's death, Engels, in a letter to J. Block, seems to soften the determinism of his and Marx's materialistic conception of history. He writes that ". . . according to the materialist conception of history, the *ultimate* determining element in history is the production and reproduction of real life. More than this neither Marx nor I have ever asserted."[16] For people to distort this by saying that the "economic element" is the only determining factor, he says, "transforms that proposition into a meaningless, abstract, senseless phrase."[17]

Economics is at the base of the situation facing mankind, but struggles in the brain—political, juristic, philosophic, and religious (plus their dogmas)—exercise their influence on history. Further, endless hosts of accidents contribute to a historical outcome. "We make our history ourselves, but, in the first place, under definite assumptions and conditions. Among these the economic ones are ultimately decisive. But the political ones . . . play a part also, but not the decisive one."[18] Further, history is made in such a way that the final results arise from conflicts between many individual wills. There are innumerable interactive forces, each of which contributes to the net result. Engels admits that he and Marx overemphasized the economic approach so as to bring it more forcefully to the attention of others. "Marx and I are ourselves partly to blame for the fact that the younger people sometimes lay more stress on the economic side than is due to it."[19]

Commodity Fetishism

Marx believed that he was demystifying capitalism. Part of that effort was the demystification of the capitalist process of production and exchange, stripping the observed but misleading reality of an ordinary item as a produced commodity. To understand the true nature of a commodity is to understand that behind every commodity is human effort.

In *Capital* Marx is extraordinarily clear in defining and describing what he means by the term *commodity fetishism*. It is worth reading in its entirety:

"A commodity appears, at first sight, a very trivial thing, and easily understood. Its analysis shows that it is, in reality, a very queer thing, abounding in metaphysical subtleties and theological niceties. So far as it is a value in use, there is nothing mysterious about it, whether we consider it from the point of view that by its properties it is capable of satisfying human wants, or from the point that those properties are the product of human labor. It is as clear as noon-day, that man, by his industry, changes the forms of the materials furnished by nature, in such a way as to make them useful to him. The form of wood, for instance, is altered by making a table out of it. Yet, for all that the table continues to be that common, everyday thing, wood. But, so soon as it steps forth as a commodity, it is changed into something transcendent. It not only stands with its feet on the ground, but, in relation to all other commodities, it stands on its head, and evolves out of its wooden brain grotesque ideas, far more wonderful than 'table-turning' ever was.

"The mystical character of commodities does not originate, therefore, in their use-value. . . . For, in the first place, however varied the useful kinds of labor or productive activities may be, it is a physiological fact, that they are functions of the human organism, and that each such function, whatever may be its nature or form, is essentially the expenditure of human brain, nerves, muscles, and so forth.

"Secondly, with regard to that which forms the groundwork for the quantitative determination of value, namely, the duration of that expenditure, or the quantity of labor, it is quite clear that there is a palpable difference between its quantity and quality. In all states of society, the labor time that it costs to produce the means of subsistence must necessarily be an object of interest to mankind, though not of equal interest in different stages of development. And lastly, from the moment that men . . . work for another, their labor assumes a social form.

"Whence, then, arises the enigmatical character of the product of labor, so soon as it assumes the form of commodities? Clearly from this form itself. The equality of all sorts of human labor is expressed objectively by their products. . . . The mutual relations of the producers, within which the social character of their labor affirmed itself, take the form of a social relation between the products.

"A commodity is . . . a mysterious thing simply because it is the social character of men's labor that appears to them as an objective character stamped upon the product of that labor; because the relation of the producers to the sum total of their own labor is presented to them as a social relation, existing not between themselves, but between the products of their labor. This is the reason why the products of labor become commodities, social things whose qualities are at the same time perceptible and imperceptible by the senses. . . . There is a definite social relation between men, that assumes, in their eyes, the fantastic form of a relation between things [products]. . . . So it is in the world of commodities [that we deal] with the products of men's hands. This I call Fetishism which attaches itself to products of labor, so soon as they are produced as commodities, and which is therefore inseparable from the production of commodities.

"This Fetishism of commodities has its origin . . . in the peculiar social character of the labor that produces them. As a general rule, articles of utility become commodities only because they are products of the labor of private individuals or groups of individuals who carry on their work independently of each other. The sum total of labor of all these private individuals forms the aggregate labor of society. Since the producers do not come into social contact with each other until they exchange their products, the specific social character of each producer's labor does not show itself except in the act of exchange. In other words, the labor of the individual asserts itself as a part of the labor of society, only by means of the relations which the act of exchange establishes directly between the products, and indirectly, through them, between the producers. To the latter, therefore, the relations connecting the labor of one individual with that of the rest appear, not as direct social relations between individuals as work, but as what they really are, material relations between persons and social relations between things."[20]

What Materialism Is and Is Not

Engels argues that materialism has been contrasted with idealism conceived as ethical or ideal goals. Idealism is then defined to involve a belief in progress, compassion, love, and an enthusiasm for truth. But he maintains that a correct understanding of Hegel's idealism will show that it has nothing to do with ideal goals; it refers to conceptions of reality that occur only in the brain. However, those who see idealism as the pursuit of ethical goals falsely contrast it with materialism, unjustly accusing materialists of glorifying "gluttony, drunkenness, lust of the eye, lust of the flesh, arrogance, cupidity, avarice, covetousness, profit-hunting and stock exchange swindling—in short, all the filthy vices in which [the Philistine] indulges in private."[21]

The basic framework of the Marxist System derives from Hegel's conception of the world as constantly changing, moving in a progressive direction toward an ultimate goal. For Marx the materialist concept that the world is a real place, where human beings are as much a part of the natural order as are rocks, plants, and animals, was hardly a new insight; he credits Feuerbach with it. Nor was it a new idea that people are what their history and culture make them. It was certainly widely held among scientifically minded people that neither the earth nor humans were necessarily special creations of God. Even the concept of a world in motion, never at rest, had been popularized by Isaac Newton. What Hegel had added was perception of the *process* (dialectic) and the *motive* (alienation) by which change occurred. Hegel also extended the religious idea that God had created humans for His purposes to the idea that God had assigned history the task of unifying people with Him. Marx accepted the idea that "history" had purpose, but the purpose was to create humans capable of full self-development and happiness, an idea that was in the air during Marx's youth and was a legacy of the Enlightenment.

For Marx the insight that although history had a purpose, that purpose worked itself out in a "real," that is, an objective natural world, had a number of corollaries: One was that the material world included ideas and beliefs, products of a material brain as well as human institutions. A second corollary was that the idea of an afterlife and of a preexisting soul residing in the body but separate from the body was also a construction of the all-too-material brain. For our purposes, the third corollary is important. Since it is human beings rather than abstract nature that make the world change, history is in the hands of human beings rather than in the hands of fate or God.

Summary

Marx and Engels emphasize the primacy of economic affairs in the determination of historical outcomes. Economic elements are more than technology; they include the methods of exchange and distribution. They emphasize the differences in historical outcomes based on different objective conditions found in each society. In his famous letter to Block, Engels tends to play down what had become for Marx's followers a kind of economic determinism. The burden of evidence is that Marx and Engels were more than economic determinists who believed that technological change determines power relationships. However, confusion on that point is not surprising.

In the Marxist System, social change is brought about by human actors. The actors are not individuals but groups whose interests are in conflict. Confusion arises as to the basic cause of social change because Marx's emphasis on classes does not fit nicely with his theory of historical materialism. Class analysis presumes a conflict of interest over the proceeds of output (national income) between those who must cooperate in the productive process—workers and owners—in a capitalist system.

Marx's example of class struggle in the *Manifesto* is the struggle of the landed aristocracy with the bourgeoisie. For several centuries agriculture as a source of income and power was declining, trade and manufacturing rising. Both aristocrat and businessman were masters. These two groups of owners struggled with each other, according to Marx, for political domination. The newer "technologies" won over the older.

Marx does not argue that the new industrial technology begot a struggle between landowners and peasants that brought into being the bourgeoisie, although both his materialist theory of history and his emphasis on the dialectic process suggest that.

Despite all, Marx insists, particularly in the *Manifesto*, that changes in modes of production create social classes. The conflict of exploiting and exploited classes is central to the Marxist System, as chapter 7 shows.

CHAPTER 7

THE ECONOMIC INTERPRETATION OF HISTORY — CLASSES

Classes are central to the Marxist System. The relations of production among persons are only significant in that they express power relations. And power relationships mean class relationships. In this chapter we see that, however persons in the social system interact, they interact as class members.

Marx learned his economics from David Ricardo. It was Ricardo who most fully developed the labor theory of value, the theory widely held during the first half of the nineteenth century that postulated that the price of a commodity, in the long run, depended upon the amount of labor time embodied in it. Marx, as we see in chapters 9 and 10, makes that theory central to his explanation of the fate of capitalism. Marx also makes use of the labor theory in his explication of how social classes are formed. Indeed, he accepts Ricardo's view that "Political Economy . . . [is] an inquiry into the laws which determine the division of the produce of industry amongst the classes who concur in its formation." That is, he accepts that economics is not primarily about the production of commodities but about the distribution of income.

Marx sees a capitalist economic system not as a way of efficiently producing goods and services to serve human wants, but rather as a political device for ordering human relationships for the purpose of allocating wealth and power. His followers so see it today. Class relationships are the human relationships that derive from the income and wealth distributed by the economic system.

Social Classes

Marx analyzes the formation of social classes this way: People are forced by necessity and against their will to play specific roles in the economy. At every stage of economic development, there arises a unique economic structure, an economic system. Along with that economic system goes a supporting political and social structure that Marx called the "superstructure" (see chapter 8). How people relate to an economic system depends upon how they relate to the sources of power in that system. In feudal times power resided with the landlord. Landlord dominated peasant. In modern times power has been transferred to the capitalist, the owner of the means of production. The laborer, owning no capital, possessing only his labor power, must sell it to the owner of capital. The supporting superstructure provides the legal and other institutional supports that are consistent with the economic system. The source of the bourgeoisie's beliefs in its right to dominate is its class position. It exists, therefore it is right. The proletariat is fooled temporarily by the myths promulgated by the official value system. To the naked eye, there appears to be a struggle between two antagonistic forces, two opposing classes with opposing interests.

However, behind class conflict hides another reality. The powerful and powerless, the bourgeoisie and proletariat, are two sides of a whole, each dependent upon the other, each locked in mortal combat with the other, both alienated from themselves and each other. Although a member of one class stands in an antagonistic relationship with a member of another class with respect to power, both are locked in a mutually supportive embrace. They have a symbiotic relationship. "Private property as wealth" fights to *preserve* its existence. To do so it must preserve the existence of the proletariat. The proletariat is compelled to *abolish* itself. To do so it must abolish the bourgeoisie, the holders of private property. The bourgeoisie enjoys its alienation, the proletariat is miserable. It is the *historic role* of the proletariat to fulfill the promise of history to abolish the bourgeoisie and therefore itself in the process of abolishing the capitalist system. It thereby ends alienation.

Here we have a problem. The proletariat, as the bearer of a humane civilization, must act self-consciously to liberate itself. First, it must realize its mission, become self-aware. Second, it must destroy what is left of its miserable living conditions, its poverty of body as well as soul. How does the proletariat become convinced that it must destroy its tormentor even though in the act it destroys itself? Marx's answer is that it becomes self-aware by suffering. "Not in vain does it go through the harsh but hardening school of labor." It does not matter what the proletariat envisions as its goal, it matters what the proletariat actually is, and according to that being, what it is historically compelled to do. Its real-life situation dictates its mission. The proletariat has *no choice* but to liberate itself.

Marx shows how each method of production creates a unique set of politico-economic relationships during particular historical periods.

Political Economy and the Class System

Marx uses the term *political economy* as we use the term *economics* today. It describes the laws governing "production and exchange of the material means of subsistence in human society."[1]

Marx insists that economic systems cannot be the same for all countries, or anywhere from generation to generation. The implications of production and exchange of the bow and arrow are far different from those of the steam engine, the mechanical loom, and the Bank of England. Political economy is therefore a "historical science" dealing with changing phenomena. Each element of exchange and production must be investigated on its own. Generally, Marx's historical view of economics is consistent with the German romantic philosophical tradition's antitheoretical stance, which was also held by German historical economists of the nineteenth century.

However, Marx, also a student of the theoretical English economist David Ricardo, concedes that out of his economic investigations will come a few general theories that will hold good for exchange and production everywhere and at every time. Marx provides as an example of a permanently important contribution to the laws of exchange and production the introduction of metallic money. Its introduction had far-reaching consequences and "brought into operation a series of laws which remain valid for all countries and historical epochs in which metallic money is a medium of exchange."[2]

The mode of production and exchange in a particular historical setting, and particular historical conditions that have "given birth" to this society, "determine the modes of distribution of its products." In tribal or communal ownership, distribution is fairly equal. Where large inequalities of distribution set in, the community is in the process of dissolution. Large- and small-scale agriculture have different degrees of equality depending on the historical conditions of their development. But large-scale farming creates class antagonism, slaveowners and slaves, feudal lords and serfs, capitalists and wage workers. Small-scale agriculture does not necessarily develop this way.

To Marx, however, the introduction of metallic money always is associated with a more or less rapid dissolution of small holdings, and the conflict between rich and poor becomes quickly pronounced.

It is with *differences in distribution* that class differences emerge: privileged and dispossessed, exploiters and exploited, rulers and ruled. Marx refers to the distribution of an *economic surplus,* derived from the surplus value of labor to a social, not *functional,* distribution, which, in neoclassical economics, is a payment to a factor of production (land, labor, or capital) for its service in production. The state emerges to protect the interests of the rulers. Distribution is not the passive result of production and exchange. Changes in forms do not automatically develop with changes in exchange and production. Old forms can remain for hundreds of years. Thus the relationship of the underlying economic structure to other social institutions may be delayed.

Nevertheless, historically, under capitalism, the distribution of property has been concentrated in the hands of a few. At the same time concentration of the propertyless masses in big towns has brought about the downfall of a centuries-old society in the space of a very few years.

The relationship between distribution of wealth and the well-being of a society causes no problems if the economy is growing, if all appear to be doing well. Only when "the mode of production" is downward, when its contribution to living standards is beyond its optimum, when increasing inequality of distribution appears unjust, are appeals made to eternal justice. In actuality, appeals to morality and justice do no good; moral indignation, however justified, cannot replace the science of economic analysis. Moral indignation only reflects the underlying decay of capitalism.[3] Indeed, the function of economic science is to demonstrate that instances of inequality are already undermining the social structure and only new methods of production and exchange will put an end to such abuses.

In its present state so-called economic science is limited to a critique of feudal survivals of production and exchange. It is the true role of science to illuminate the socialist critique of capitalist production, then make clear how more and more intolerable the fetters on production are becoming—the antagonism, the exploitation, the constant divergence of wealthy and poor—and how the colossal productive forces created by capitalism only await revolution to become part of a cooperative society of work on a planned basis. Only a planned economy is capable of ensuring to all members of society a way by which individuals can develop their capacities more and more fully.[4]

Marx asserts that social scientists fail to see that economic relations go far beyond simple production and distribution and engulf all of social life, entering every human relationship. Capitalism has the ability to create misery as well as economic growth. That is why critics of capitalism cannot simply "talk economics." They must talk of every aspect of social life if economic matters are to be properly understood.

The "Free Laborer"

In feudal times laborers were attached to the land. They had a right to life, a right to subsistence income. But they were not free. Marx believes that capitalism liberated workers from one form of serfdom only to reenslave them in another. Under feudalism no free labor market existed and capitalism could not develop.

Capitalism, Marx argues, was made possible only when the owner of money could find labor power for sale as a commodity. Laborers must own no property from which they earn money. Labor power appears on the market as a commodity that it can sell. A laborer must be the untrammeled owner of his own labor power. He cannot be allowed to sell himself into slavery; that would convert him from the owner of a commodity into a commodity. The system of free labor power permits capitalism to maintain separation, on a continuous basis, of the worker from the means of production and to keep immediate producers as wage laborers.

After economic conditions have transformed the mass of people of a country into wage workers and the domination of capital has created for these people a common situation with common interests, we have a social class opposed to capital but not yet united, as a class, for the political struggle.[5]

Until the proletariat is sufficiently "developed" to constitute a class, the struggle between the bourgeoisie and proletariat cannot enter its political phase. As time passes, the struggle becomes more clearly defined, and the proletariat is able to see for itself where it stands. As long as "they see in poverty only poverty," and do not see the revolutionary subversive side, they will do nothing. But as soon as scientific understanding is produced by those who understand historical movements and provide the proletariat with full knowledge of the facts, the situation ceases to be simply abstract or doctrinaire and becomes revolutionary.[6]

The Class Struggle of the Bourgeoisie and the Proletariat

Marx's most evocative description of the nature of the class struggle is contained in *The Manifesto of the Communist Party*. Marx and Engels proclaim the history of all previously existing societies is the history of class struggles between oppressor and oppressed. Sometimes the fights are hidden, sometimes in the open. The outcome each time ends in either a revolutionary reconstitution of society at large or the ruin of the contending classes. This is his analysis.

In all historical epochs we find a complicated arrangement of society into various orders, graded by social rank. In Rome there were patricians, knights, plebeians, slaves; in the Middle Ages, feudal lords, vassals, guild masters, journeymen, apprentices, serfs.

Modern bourgeois society, sprouting from the ruins of feudal society, has not abolished class antagonisms. In fact, it has established new classes, new conditions of oppression, and new forms of struggle in place of old ones.

The bourgeois epoch is different from many of its predecessors. Instead of a variety of hostile camps facing one another in societies that are organized in a variety of ways, the world has been greatly simplified. There now exist only two great camps: bourgeois and proletarian.

The bourgeoisie derived from the chartered burghers of the earliest towns. The discovery of America, colonial trade, and considerable increases in the means of exchange all led to commerce, navigation, industrial growth, and thereby rapidly to the revolutionary element in the tottering feudal society.

Manufacturing systems replaced guilds with their narrow markets. The division of labor in corporate guilds vanished in the face of the division of labor in each single workshop set up by manufacturers.

Markets grew, demand rose; small manufacture was insufficient. Steam and machinery revolutionized industrial production. Modern industry replaced manufacturing and the industrial middle class. Industrial millionaires, the leaders of "whole industrial armies, make up the modern bourgeoisie."[7]

Modern industry established the world market for which the discovery of America paved the way. The market spurred immense development in commerce, in navigation, in land communication. This in turn reacted on the growth of industry—and along with it the growth of navigation and railway extension. All social classes surviving from the Middle Ages were pushed aside. The development of the bourgeoisie was itself the culmination of a long historical process. As the bourgeois class grew to prominence, so did its political power. It first allied itself everywhere with urban republics, monarchies, or semifeudal institutions. It finally overthrew all encumbrances of feudalism and took charge of the state, so that "the executive of the modern state is but a committee for managing the common affairs of the whole bourgeoisie."[8]

Once the bourgeois class was ascendant, it ended all feudal, patriarchal, idyllic relations. "It has pitilessly torn asunder the motley feudal ties that bound man to his 'natural superiors' and has left remaining no other nexus between man and man than naked self-interest, callous cash payment."[9]

"Philistine sentimentalism, . . . [has changed] all personal worth into exchange value, and in place of the numerous indefeasible chartered freedoms, has set up that single, unconscionable freedom—Free Trade. In one word, for exploitation, veiled by religious and political illusions, it has substituted naked, shameless, direct, brutal exploitation."[10] All men of science, priests and poets are now wage laborers. The sentimental veil of family relationships has been stripped away, leaving mere money relationships.

Yet the bourgeoisie display "brutal vigor." Their wonders of human achievement surpass the pyramids, Roman aqueducts, Gothic cathedrals. The bourgeoisie live by constantly revolutionizing the instruments of production and thereby the relations of production, and along with them whole relations of society. "All that is solid melts into air, all that is holy is profaned, and man is at last compelled to face with sober senses, his real conditions of life, and his relations with his kind."[11]

The needs of constantly expanding markets for its products spreads bourgeois society over the world. By exploiting all markets it gives "cosmopolitan character to production and consumption" everywhere. It undermines the very ground upon which reaction stands, dislodges old industries, introducing life-and-death questions for all civilizations. Raw materials are dug up from every quarter of the globe; old wants are denied, new wants are created.

National onesidedness and narrowmindedness become more and more impossible. World literature arises from local literatures. International uniformity of social and political life arises from the global changes created by the spread of capitalism throughout the world.

Commodities cheapened by improved means of production and communication bring down "all Chinese walls," forcing the barbarians against their will to capitulate "on pain of extinction."

The bourgeoisie concentrates population, production, and property. Economic concentration usually means centralized means of production and ultimately political concentration. Independent or loosely connected provinces "with separate interests, laws, governments and systems of taxation, became lumped together into one nation, with one government, one code of laws, one national class-interest, one frontier and one customs tariff."[12]

The productive capacity of the bourgeoisie is further celebrated by Marx: ". . . during its rule of scarce one hundred years, [the bourgeois class] has created more massive and more colossal production forces than have all preceding generations together."[13] Man has subdued nature's forces through the development of machinery, chemistry, agriculture, steam navigation, railways, electric telegraphs, and by "clearing of whole continents for cultivation, canalization of rivers . . . [what] earlier century had even a presentiment that such productive forces slumbered in the lap of social labor?"[14]

Free competition replaced feudal forces, which were no longer compatible with the forces of industrialism. The social and political constitution adapted to free competition and to the new economic and political sway of the bourgeois class.

Yet periodical commercial crises threaten bourgeois society and previously created productive forces. The reason for these returns to barbarism every so often is that the conditions of the bourgeois society are too narrow to confine the wealth that created them. On the one hand, there is an enforced destruction of a mass of productive forces; and on the other, new markets are conquered and the old ones are more thoroughly exploited: "by paving the way for more extensive and more destructive crises, and by diminishing the means whereby crises are prevented."[15]

The weapons used by the bourgeoisie to destroy feudalism are turned against the bourgeois class itself. Certainly the most destructive weapon that the bourgeoisie have created to turn against themselves is the modern working class, the proletariat. The proletariat is developed in proportion to the development of the bourgeoisie. Its members live and die according to the vicissitudes of the bourgeoisie. The proletarian worker becomes an appendage to the machine. He is paid only the value of his subsistence, enough for his maintenance and for the propagation of his race. His work may be speeded up to speed up the production of subsistence, thereby lowering the wage. The pace of his work is determined by the speed of the machine.

Skills decline as machines become more proficient. The differences of sex and strength go by the board. The lower strata of the middle class sink gradually into the proletariat. The net effect is that the proletariat not only increases in numbers but concentrates in great masses.

Attempts by workers to organize usually fail. Victory in strikes is not the main point. The main point is that the proletariat grows in self-awareness by means of the class struggle; that the proletariat organizes into stronger, firmer, and mightier political organizations, operating in its own interests.

As the final class struggle nears its decisive hour, all other existing classes stand with the bourgeoisie but face the united proletariat. The lower middle class, the small manufacturer, and the peasant all fight against the bourgeoisie to save themselves from extinction. They are not revolutionary but conservative, indeed reactionary. This is the "dangerous class," some of which may be swept into the proletariat revolution; the bulk of that class becomes "part of a bribed tool of reactionary intrigue."

Thus the role of the proletariat as the bearer of revolution and the vanguard of the new society is clarified. The proletariat is forced by circumstance to become self-aware, that is, to become conscious of itself as a class. Members of the proletariat are the only people capable of seeing reality clearly. They solidify into a class movement. The remaining opponents, the few remaining capitalists with something to lose and the lower middle classes who still suffer from ideological blindness, are easily swept away. The fall of the capitalist class and victory of the proletariat are equally inevitable.[16]

Summary

The Marxist System abstracts from the variety of interest groups that Marx recognizes and emphasizes the two that, for him, are most important because of the dynamic role they play in social change. He also sees the two classes as increasingly polarized. As capitalism increases social wealth, it increases the misery of the proletariat. Accepting the Hegelian dialectical version of progress as one requiring conflict, he sees no possibility of shared interests and common purposes.

The dynamics of social change require the evolution of the proletariat from an economic class "in itself," a mass of industrial workers that find themselves dispossessed, to a politically sophisticated class "for itself" united by growing despair. It is only when they become "self-conscious" that they can be mobilized to liberate themselves.

At the outset of capitalism, Marx's concept of class is objective and functional. That is, the observer can see the class of an individual by investigating the actor's economic function. Actors themselves may not recognize their social place. Later both classes recognize their locations and class becomes a subjective category as well.

The early Marx of the *Philosophic and Economic Manuscripts of 1844* and the later Marx of *Capital* converge with his discussion of social class. The division of labor and specialization were, according to the *Manuscripts,* the root causes of alienation. They are also the the sources of social classes. In order to eliminate alienation, it is necessary to eliminate the division of labor. The division of labor can be eliminated only when capitalism and the class structure that it spawns disappear.

The Marxist System encompasses all of social life. Economic relationships do not stand alone. Social class, in the long run, determines all social relationships. Under capitalism, as under all social and economic systems, there must be a correspondence among all elements of the culture. The economic system requires supportive institutions—law, ideology, family, religion, and so forth. These institutions are called the superstructure, which provides aid to the underlying substructures (the modes of production) to maintain the hegemony of capitalism until the system finally destroys itself. Chapter 8 discusses the superstructure

CHAPTER 8

THE SUPERSTRUCTURE

The Marxist System holds that among the institutions necessary to support the edifice of capitalism are ideology, the state, religion, marriage and the family, and civil liberties. The first thing to understand is that even as nebulous a concept as "ideology" is material from the Marxist point of view. Ideas are as real as commodities.

Because they are material or real things, they have significant influence on events, and to survive over time they must be useful to the maintenance of the existing reality. It is tempting to say that they are "determined" by the substructure, but that suggests too close a cause-and-effect relationship. Super-structural elements may evolve with changing needs, or they may die gradually if they prove to be nonfunctional. They also interact to change the substructure. Following is a brief discussion of each of the major elements of the super-structure.

Ideology

Just as people learn new skills in order to earn a living as the nature of the economy changes, so their ideas about the real world change. Therefore ideas are transitory, even ephemeral, with respect to underlying realities. On the other hand, ideas may last well beyond their period of usefulness and, indeed, may hinder the growth of new understanding. For Marx, the concept of ideology is one of a *false* conception of reality. The bourgeoisie are prone to the error of regarding what appears "good" for them to be good for the entire society. Persons with "subversive" ideas are not simply wrong; they are dangerously wrong. For Marx, only the proletariat, with the help of revolutionary intellectuals, can see the world in its proper perspective.

The usefulness of the bourgeois form of self-deception as far as the status quo is concerned is that it can be widely promulgated, used as a justification to anesthetize the proletariat and deceive the bourgeoisie into believing that what they hold is not only a correct but an eternally valuable perception of reality.

The State

ITS ORIGINS

Engels describes the origins of the state as being in primitive tribal organizations that were run communistically, citing the social organization of the Iroquois Indians and tribes in ancient Greece. In these complex societies, decisions were made and quarrels mediated by the group as a whole. Since among Indians there were no inheritance or property rights to protect, all affairs ran "smoothly without soldiers, gendarmes or police; without nobles, kings, governors, prefects or judges; without prisons; without trials."[1] In America, the 1500-year-old "gentile" (heathen) society was destroyed to make a new "civilization," which was ushered in by "theft, rape, deceit, and treachery."

In Greece, in the "Heroic Age," the tribal system was still vigorous, but in process of dissolution. Population increases, growth of herds, field agriculture, and handicrafts arose, creating differences in wealth. There was considerable warfare for both land and slaves. Wealth was "praised," hereditary nobility began to develop, and war for profit undermined the older "gentile" society.* To protect the new class of property owners, since tribal forms forbade private property, a new institution was invented, the state. Thus Engels's distinction between the state and society is that the state is a creation of the class system, society a natural human organization.

THE STATE AND PROPERTY

In its initial form in the tribal world, property was by necessity communal. Several tribes lived together, and the right to property was mere possession. In the Middle Ages, property moved by stages to movable property and manufactured capital to modern capital determined by big industry and universal competition. Modern private property corresponds to the modern state. No longer an estate but a class, the bourgeoisie is organized nationally, not locally. "Through the emancipation of private property from the community, the State becomes a separate entity, beside and outside civil society; but is

---

*Engels discusses gens, phratry, and tribes, following Lewis Morgan, the American anthropologist. Gens are subdivisions of a tribe, based on kinship. A phratry is a group of gens; a tribe, a group of phratries.

nothing more than the form of organization which the bourgeois necessarily adapt both for internal and external purposes."[2] Non-Marxist French, English, and American writers agree, according to Marx, that the state exists for the sake of private property.

THE STATE—AND THE RULING CLASS

The state presents itself as an "ideological power" over man. Society creates for itself an organization for safeguarding common interests against internal and external threats. The state becomes an independent organ of a particular class, enforcing its supremacy. Even when the state is defending the entire society, it is really defending a particular class. As the state becomes an independent power it produces a "further ideology." It legitimizes private law, laws protecting private property. All laws, those that deal with private property and those that do not, are made internally consistent to eliminate all inner contradictions.[3]

THE STATE—ITS FUTURE

The state has not existed for all time. Many societies have done without it. Its development has come because of the cleavage of the society into classes. When production is organized on "a free and equal association of producers" the state will disappear because it will no longer be needed. It will become a historical exhibit in "the museum of antiquities."

THE STATE—ECONOMIC GROWTH AND THE LAW

The state can either encourage growth through speeding development or it can oppose development, in which case it will destroy itself. Alternatively it can prevent economic development from proceeding along some lines and help society develop along others. In the last two instances political power can do a great deal of harm and waste energy and material. When the state engages in war, economic development can be ruined, and often the vanquished gains more than the conqueror.

As soon as a new division of labor is opened, new kinds of professional lawyers develop. They are necessary to help harmonize general economic conditions with the state and to reduce the contradictions within the state between the economy and the law. This involves ridding society of anticombination (antitrust) laws that get in the way of growth.

Religion

For Marx, religion is nothing but the reflection in people's minds of their fear and ignorance of the forces that control their lives. Religion helps people deal with the inexplicable mysteries of the forces of nature. Sometimes the powers people worship represent natural forces; at other times, power is transferred to *one* almighty God, who is but a reflection of the abstract man. Monotheism was the vulgarized philosophy of later Greeks and found its "incarnation in the exclusively national god of the Jews." Such a god is a "convenient, handy and universally adaptable form" as long as people remain under the control of the forces, natural and social, that dominate them. We have consistently seen that economic forces dominate people.[4] "Bourgeois economics can neither prevent crises in general, nor protect the individual capitalists from losses, bad debts and bankruptcy, nor secure the individual workers against unemployment and destitution. It is still true that man proposes and God (that is, the alien domination of the capitalist mode of production) disposes."[5]

However, when society brings such forces under domination by taking possession of all means of production, society will then be freed from the bondage of alien forces. Then, man will dispose: "Only then will the last alien force which is still reflected in religion vanish; and with it will also vanish the religious reflection itself, for the simple reason that then there will be nothing left to reflect."[6]

Religion arose in all primitive times from erroneous conceptions about man's own nature and the nature around him. Since the material conditions of life determine religious notions, just as any other notions men have, their conceptions will be as varied as their life experiences.

"*Religious* misery is at one and the same time the *expression* of the real misery and protestations against real misery. Religion is the sigh of the oppressed creature, the mind of the heathen world, as it is the spirit of unspiritual conditions. It is the opiate of the people. . . . The removal of religion as illusory happiness . . . is the requirement of their real happiness . . . the criticism of religion is therefore basically the criticism of the *vale of tears* whose halo is religion."[7]

"The task of history, after the world beyond truth has disappeared [is] to establish the truth of this world. . . . After the 'saint-image' of man's self-alienation has been unmasked . . . the criticism of heaven thus changes into the criticism of [this] earth, the criticism of religion into the criticism of justice, the criticism of theology into the criticism of politics."[8]

Marriage

There are three chief forms of marriage conforming to the three steps in human development: (1) under savagery, group marriage; (2) under barbarism, pairing marriage; (3) under civilization, monogamy. In the upper stage of barbarism, between pairing marriage and monogamy, occurs the domination of men over female slaves and the practice of polygamy.

With the rise of the bourgeoisie, all forms of human relationships change. Arranged marriages give way to contractual marriages. The principle of freely contracting individuals in a capitalist market society extends to family formation. Group marriage disappears; monogamy gains ascendancy. Mutual inclination, or love, becomes the basis of marital partnership, not an appraisal of each other's financial situation, at least as a matter of principle. Matrimony, although a legal affair, becomes voluntary. Indeed only marriage based on free choice of partners is proclaimed moral by "religious authorities," according to Marx.

Engels says that love marriage has become a human right, not only for men but for women as well. But, he notes that, curiously, whereas the depressed classes are denied other human rights directly or indirectly, they enjoy free marital choice to a greater extent than do the ruling classes.

The bourgeoisie, primarily motivated by economic considerations, tend not to enjoy freedom of voluntary choice in marriage. Financial considerations similar to those at work during the Middle Ages tend to dictate choice of partners.

In the upper classes, failure to choose marriage partners voluntarily, based on love, leads to "prostitution" among women. It also leads to infidelity among men who have chosen wives for economic reasons rather than mutual affection.

In our day of capitalist production, the more sexual freedom is translated into open prostitution, the more demoralizing are its effects. It demoralizes men more than women. For only those women practicing prostitution are degraded, and to a lesser degree than is usually believed; but the character of the whole male world is degraded by prostitution. Engels adds, "In nine cases out of ten, a long engagement is practically a preparatory school for conjugal infidelity."[9]

We are in the process of a social revolution that will undermine the foundations of monogamy and along with it prostitution (the handmaiden of monogamy). Monogamy arose out of the need for men to concentrate their property, for inheritance purposes, in their children. "For this purpose monogamy was essential on the woman's part," but not the man's. Men's promiscuity necessitated women's monogamy to assure legitimate parenthood for inheritance purposes. In the impending revolution, most material means of production will go to the state, reducing anxiety about inheritance to a minimum.

Engels asks rhetorically: "Since monogamy rose from economic causes, will it disappear when the causes disappear?" It won't, Engels responds. It will be more "completely realized." Prostitution will disappear because a "statistically calculable" number of women will no longer need to sell their bodies for money. They will undertake productive work. Monogamy will become a reality for men as well as women.

Indeed, the position of men and women will change. With the means of production being common property, the family will cease to be the economic unit of society. The care and education of children will become a social affair. Since both legitimate and illegitimate children will be treated equally by society, there will be no fear of "consequences," thus a "girl" will feel able to participate in "more unrestrained sexual intercourse" with the "man she loves." This full freedom in or out of marriage will become operative only with the abolition of capitalist production and the property relations created by it. Engels says that monogamy, the natural condition of man, will be achieved, along with equality of women, and there will be an end to infidelity.

Civil Liberties

Marx's discussion of civil liberties arises in the context of the "Jewish Question" debated in Europe from the time of the French Revolution. Bruno Bauer takes the view that Jews cannot receive full citizenship when their religious habits (e.g., the injunction against work on the Sabbath) prevent full citizen participation.

Thus, Marx notes, the Jew must give up his religion to meet Bauer's standard. In Germany, where at that time there was no single state but all principalities considered themselves Christian, the issue is a theological one. In the United States, where there is no state religion, the issue is political. Social criticism does not take the form of religious criticism. "Criticism then becomes a criticism of the political state."

Marx's response is consistent with his views on religion and the class struggle. If, in a secular state, religion of any kind flowers, it is because the need for religion has not disappeared. Religion is a "defect." The religious "small-mindedness of free citizens [is derived] from their general small-mindedness. We do not maintain that they must abolish their religious limitations in order to abolish their human limitations. We do not turn secular human problems into religious ones; we turn religious questions into secular ones."[10]

This is where Marx stands: "The political emancipation of the Jew, the Christian, or the religious man in general is a question of the emancipation of the state from Judaism, Christianity and religion in general." This also means that even a religion-free state, where all are citizens with equal rights, will not emancipate man from religion or any other artificial relationship. "Human emancipation is achieved only when the individual gives up being an abstract citizen and becomes a member of a species as individual man in his daily life and work and situation, when he recognizes and organizes his *forces proper*, his own strength, as part of the forces of society, which are then no longer separated from him as a political power."[11] The precondition for the end of religion is the end of capitalist exploitation.

For Marx, all people are slaves even in a civil society, although they may be free in appearance. As long as people are alienated in bourgeois society, they will never be free. The lack of religious freedom is simply part of the slavery that people endure in modern society.

Summary

It is important to keep in mind that the Marxist System is holistic. All the institutions of society must be consistent with the interests of the ruling class. Ideology must support the myths of the rightness of political power's location. The family structure must be harmonious with underlying economic realities. Religion is supportive of the power structure by providing an "opiate," a temporary balm to the hurt that the social order inflicts. Even civil liberties are false liberties. People are freed from, say, religious persecution, but are still enslaved to the larger sociopolitical system. And the state, which passes laws and administers justice, is never neutral. Even when it appears to make concessions to the less fortunate, the concessions are simply ways of keeping social peace while preserving the basic economic system.

The Marxist System provides a complete framework with which to understand the historical context in which the process of social change occurs. Marxism provides motivation for change and indicates the direction that it will take. Beyond that, Marx does not go. He does not attempt to provide a detailed description of the socialist and communist systems that he anticipates will develop when the historical process of change comes to an end. In each location there will be a unique configuration of interlocking social institutions, the one supporting the other.

Whereas Marx willingly charts the course of capitalist destruction to its end, he is consistent when he refuses to specify the nature of new supporting institutions. It is an interesting speculative question as to what institutions will be necessary in a world without conflicts to adjust. He is clear that the state will disappear, religion will be obsolete, marital relationships will be "natural," apparently requiring no formal institutional arrangements to assure the inheritance of family name and property that "men" have historically demanded. The protection of civil rights will be unnecessary. Ideology, a distorted view of oneself and the objective world, will be no more.

Social change depends on the modes of production and the relations of production, the economic system. The relationships among institutions, their assumed interdependence, are addressed in chapter 12.

The superstructure is dependent upon the substructure, which is the economic system. Before the substructure changes, the capitalist system must complete its historic function. To demonstrate how this occurs, Marx turns to economic analysis.

The economic "model" that he uses is derived from classical economists Adam Smith and David Ricardo. We need not concern ourselves here with their arguments other than to say that Marx accepts the method of analysis, assumptions, and conclusions of David Ricardo. Two of these are central to chapters 9 and 10. The first is that the value or price of produced goods is determined by the content of the labor services contained in them. The second is that in the long run the economy will cease to grow, that is, will achieve a stationary state, one in which the living standards of workers and owners will remain unchanged.

In chapter 9 we discuss Marx's theory of value (price formation), which sets the stage for chapter 10, his theory of the self-destruction of capitalism.

CHAPTER 9

CAPITALISM: VALUE AND PRICE

In his economic model Marx shows that capitalism has three important characteristics: First is its ability to promote the accumulation of productive capacities of enormous proportions. Second is its inability to provide a mechanism
whereby all that can be produced is consumed. The third, its ultimately fatal
characteristic, is, in Marx's language, a "contradiction." As a consequence of
its success in being able to create productive capacity, capitalism destroys its
ability to make the profits necessary to continue the process of capital accumulation. The second and third characteristics create a hungry, impoverished, and
hostile army of unemployed at a time when the capitalist class, with declining
profits, is losing the rationale for its existence and the power to protect itself
in a hostile environment.

However, Marx first needs to explain why the sources of capitalist profit
and thus the amazing capacity of the capitalist system to build the foundations of the economy yet to come, one of abundance and free of alienation,
ultimately disappear. The story begins with Marx's theory of value (or price),
the subject matter of this chapter.

The Meaning of Value

A commodity has value if it meets two criteria: (1) it satisfies a human want,
and (2) it "contains" (is made with) labor power. It is not enough that a commodity, say, a diamond, is found and exchanged for money. From the Marxist
view, the diamond has a price but no value. The diamond in its rough and
unpolished state satisfies only the first criterion. It has use value, and that is
why it has a price. But goods have value in the Marxist sense only when they
have both a use and contain human labor. "If then we leave out of considera-

tion use value of commodities, they have only one common property left, that of being products of labor."[1] A commodity has value because abstract human value is embodied in it. According to Marx: "The imaginary price-form may sometimes conceal a direct or indirect real value-relation; for instance, the price of uncultivated land, which is without value, because no human labor has been incorporated in it."[2] Thus a thing with use value can command a price without having value in the Marxist sense of containing labor. Alternatively, other things having use value, such as air, command no price because they contain no labor. Marx does not refer either to uncultivated land or to air as a commodity because commodities contain labor.

SOCIALLY NECESSARY LABOR TIME
The value of a commodity is determined by the socially necessary labor time contained in it. Counted as socially necessary is only that time required for production under normal circumstances, containing the average degree of skill and intensity using modern machinery. The greater the productivity of capital, the greater the output of labor in conjunction with capital equipment; the less the labor time, the less the value of the commodity.

As an example of the exchange value of two commodities, Marx uses the example of coats and linen. He argues that in trying to understand the relative values of coats and linen, we can abstract from them their use value. We can convert different levels of skills into an average level of skill embodied in the tailoring and weaving. What is left is the quantity of human labor. The difference in the value of the two commodities must then be only the labor power expended in creating them.

Different commodities require different degrees of skill. Skilled labor is nothing more than simple labor intensified. If a skilled laborer produces twice as much in the same time as an unskilled one, his labor is worth twice that of the unskilled worker. The adjustment of the prices of the commodities to the different level of skills embodied in them is determined by market forces. The proper standard for labor power is that it must be of average efficiency; workers must be of average skill, using a normal amount of exertion. Wasted time does not add to the value of a commodity—nor does wasted material or material of unnecessarily high quality.

"Living" labor power must be combined with capital to produce linens and coats. Marx uses the term "past labor" interchangeably with capital equipment and raw materials *used up* in the process of production. In determining the value of the yarn that is woven into coats and linen, all processes previously carried on in different places to produce the cotton and the spindle used up in the process may be looked upon as past labor. All raw materials and time spent producing them must be included in the value of the yarn to the degree that they are used up in producing the yarn. Capital is nothing but "congealed" past labor *used up* in the present. The relative values of the two commodities are, then, equal to the sum of the living labor plus the used-up past labor embodied in them.[3]

DEMAND AND VALUE

Although the value of a commodity is determined by the socially necessary labor time contained in it, if there is no demand for the commodity, it has no value. Commodities must have use value.[4]

THE VALUE OF LABOR POWER

The value of labor power is determined in essentially the same manner as that of any other commodity, by the labor time necessary for its production and reproduction. The laborer must sell his labor power as a commodity in return for money. The laborer cannot sell commodities containing labor power because he has no raw materials, implements, and the like. He owns no capital goods.

Although the laborer is a free human being, he is confronted with a market that has no interest in him except insofar as his labor can contribute to the creation of a salable commodity. Only in this respect do the costs of raising, educating, and sustaining the laborer interest the market, necessitating that wages be high enough to assure the continuation of the workforce over time.

In order to obtain usable labor power, the wage (or price) of labor must be high enough to pay labor's costs of production and reproduction. Should the market pay less, the laborer will be unable to renew his vital energy and be unable to deliver the labor power necessary to produce the commodity. Without means of subsistence, the supply of labor power will decline. So, in the long run, labor must be paid a subsistence wage high enough to continually renew the source of labor power.[5]

The Theory of Exploitation

CONSTANT CAPITAL AND VARIABLE CAPITAL

Constant capital is that portion of the value of machinery and materials used up in production and added to the value of the product. Only the portion used up—depreciation and raw materials—is transferred to the value of the product. *Variable capital* is living labor power that in the form of marketable commodities reproduces the equivalent of its own value plus a surplus, which is added to the value of a commodity.

An example of constant capital would be a spinning machine with a working life of ten years. For its lifetime, a portion of its value has been transferred to the product. After ten years of service, all its value is transferred to the commodity. Its value at the end of that period is zero. If the original value of the machines was 150 or, say, 500 labor days, the machine cannot add to the commodity any more than the equivalent of 150 or 500 labor days.

Variable capital, which is living labor, transfers value to the commodity. For part of the working day, the laborer is transferring enough value to the product to pay him the cost of his subsistence. That becomes his pay. Should the laborer work for a period of time longer than is necessary to create the value of subsistence, that value is "appropriated" by the capitalist as surplus value.[6]

THE RATE OF SURPLUS VALUE

The rate of surplus value is the ratio of surplus value to wages. If, for instance, laborers work a twelve-hour day and are paid for six hours of work, the rate of surplus value (or the rate of exploitation) is 100 percent. Capitalist profit consists of appropriated surplus value and is the only source.

$$\text{Rate of Surplus Value } (S/V) = 6/6 = 100\%$$

The capitalist can extract more surplus value from living labor by reducing the labor time that it takes to pay subsistence in the following ways:

1. Children's and women's labor may be employed with the use of machinery not requiring heavy muscular exertion. More members of the family may be employed, thereby spreading the cost of the family's subsistence more widely. Labor power is now cheaper.

2. Labor's productivity may be enhanced by increasing the output of each laborer. This reduces the time needed for the laborer to create subsistence.[7]

3. The workday may be prolonged. Machines do not grow tired; they can set the pace at which workmen labor. Machinery does lose value over time because of obsolescence. Therefore, hurrying its use while it is new is a desirable strategy to earn surplus value.

4. The longer the working day, the more fully constant capital is used. Capital unused is capital wasted. Lengthening the working day for the laborer does not harm capital, so there is much to be gained.

A contradiction, in capitalist systems, Marx argues, appears when it is realized that machinery can replace labor. The contradiction is that since only living labor creates surplus value, the replacement of labor by machinery tends to be self-defeating; the source of surplus tends to dry up. According to Marx, the way out of the dilemma, discovered by "learned" and "Christian" economists of his day, was to lengthen the working day as far as humanly possible so as to compensate for the diminished number of laborers.[8]

INTENSIFICATION OF LABOR

Experience shows, says Marx, that immoderate working days lead to a reaction on the part of society, whose "very sources of life are menaced." The law intrudes in economic affairs to put limits to the working day. Capitalists, in turn, respond by increasing the intensity of work.

In England, pressure in Parliament to shorten the working day still further has tended to increase, and the results of a shortened workday have been good. The productivity of machinery has been improved in order to compensate for reduced hours of work. However, greater managerial vigilance over work habits has seen to it that no time is wasted during the shortened day. Also, piecework has been introduced, especially in industries using little labor, with the result that the workday has intensified. The results in one case reported by Marx are these: "Mr. Robert Gardiner reduced the hours of labor in his two large factories at Preston, on and after the 20th of April, 1844, from twelve to eleven hours a day." The results of about a year's working was that "the same amount of product for the same cost was received, and the work[ing] people as a whole earned in eleven hours as much as they did before in twelve."[9]

Accumulation and the Falling Rate of Profit

ORGANIC COMPOSITION OF CAPITAL

An increase in constant capital has the function of increasing the productivity of variable capital and becomes the main source of continued profit. This is so because the productivity of labor is closely connected with the quantity and quality of constant capital with which laborers work. Thus C/V, the ratio of constant to variable capital (the organic composition of capital), increases in the long run.

Marx credits Adam Smith with the fundamental insight that improved capital equipment increases labor productivity.[10] Marx agrees with Smith that the division of labor, its skills, and the productivity of land are all important sources of worker productivity.[11] But in the end, labor productivity depends on capital and the "law" of the progressive increase of capital relative to living labor.

THE FALLING RATE OF PROFIT

As the accumulation of capital proceeds, the proportion of constant to variable capital increases. This means that since C/V must rise, the rate of profit $S/(C + V)$ must decline. This decline occurs because the S can be derived only from V, variable capital. The ratio of C to V must increase, even though in absolute terms the amount of V may increase, decrease, or remain the same. Countries at different stages of development, says Marx, may have different organic compositions of capital.

According to Marx, the law of ever-increasing organic composition of capital is not so much a law as a tendency. So there is no reason that at particular times the volume of V may not be growing relative to C. In the long run the mass of constant capital will tend to grow more quickly than variable capital, so much so that the rate of profit will have the tendency to fall. It is also possible for the mass (absolute amount) of profit to rise while the rate of profit may be declining.

There are other reasons why the absolute volume of profit may increase. The process of capital accumulation may bring about an increase in the demand for variable capital relative to constant capital, thus increasing wages and encouraging marriage and reproduction. On the other hand, high wages encourage the introduction of machinery, creating unemployment. Despite strong growth in accumulation, in the long run profits will eventually fall.

When capitalists with large amounts of capital lower prices to drive out competitors and are willing to accept lower rates of profits to do so, those whom Marx calls "vulgar" economists seem to believe that business people are acting irrationally. Such economists also show their ignorance of how a capitalist economy operates when they argue that monopolists can set prices at will and earn whatever rate of profit they wish. The idea that profits are an arbitrary addition to cost involves "crude and incorrect reasoning." Market prices and profits are determined by competition. Capitalists do what they must to survive.

It is true that as capital accumulates, prices decline, and the mass (total amount) of profits increases with sales. But the all-important *rate* of profit will fall because constant capital (C) rises in relation to variable capital (V). With the proportion of living labor declining and "materialized" labor such as raw materials and wear-and-tear rising, $S/(C + V)$ must be falling because C/V is rising. Individual capitalists have no control over this phenomenon.

The progressive tendency for the capitalist's rate of profit to fall is peculiar to capitalist production because although the productivity of labor progressively increases, increased productivity cannot overcome the loss of living labor in the productive process when capital is increasing. Marx says that the rate of profit may fall for other reasons as well, but in capitalism it is a logical outcome of the increasing organic composition of capital. Since the *rate* of profit is measured by the proportion of the mass of surplus value (the total amount of profit) to the total value of invested capital, the falling rate of profit reflects the falling ratio of surplus value to total capital and is for this reason independent of any division of profit among laborers and capitalists.[12] No redistribution of income between the two classes can prevent the rate of profit from falling and thereby endangering capitalism itself.

Under competition, a fall in prices of commodities and a rise in the absolute amount of profits due to greater sales of cheapened commodities is but another phase in the relentless process by which the rate of profit declines. In short, the law of the falling rate of profit is consistent with simultaneous increases in the *amounts* of profit.[13]

Marx's argument may be shown this way:

S = surplus value (or profit)

V = variable (or living capital)

C = fixed (or used-up capital in the productive process)

$C + V + S$ = value of each commodity (or the value of all commodities, the Gross Domestic Product)

$S/(C + V)$ = rate of profit

On the basis of a simplifying assumption that $S = V$, that is, $S/V = $ 100 percent, the argument is that even if S rises (the mass of profit increases), $S/(C + V)$ will, in the long run, fall. C is determined by the value of ever-growing capital equipment in a developing economy. C will increase relatively to V (therefore S). Capital will replace labor. $C + V$ rises faster than S.

COUNTERACTING TENDENCIES

The rate of profit tends to fall in the long run. In the short run, the decline may be counteracted by (1) an increase in the intensity of exploitation, (2) a depression of wages below their value, (3) a reduction in the cost of elements of constant capital, (4) relative overpopulation, and (5) foreign trade.

An important short-run check on the decline in the rate of profit occurs when the market rate of wages is depressed below its value. Also, constant capital may be cheapened if its cost of production is reduced.

Overpopulation makes cheap labor available to new lines of production, thus making them profitable. A rising rate of profit in all industries is then possible. But now industries will be subject to the same laws of accumulation, and rates of profit will eventually decline.

Foreign trade cheapens the element of constant capital by cheapening the necessities of life and permitting the expansion of the scale of production. Foreign trade further aids capitalist development by providing an ever-expanding market.

Capital invested in foreign trade yields a higher rate of profit than a domestic investment because it competes with less highly developed production facilities so commodities can be sold above their values although sold at lower prices than those of competing countries. Labor in advanced countries may produce articles of higher quality than those produced by competing labor in backward countries, yet be paid as if they were the same quality. Also, capital invested in colonies may be highly profitable because "coolies and slaves" are easy to exploit.

EQUALIZATION OF THE RATE OF PROFIT

In a market economy where goods are sold by a variety of industries with different compositions of variable and constant capital, shoes compete with food. Items made of metal compete with those made of wood. Each firm, depending on its technical requirements, will have different organic compositions of capital. It is clear that the rate of profit, $S/(C + V)$, will be the same in industries with the same organic compositions of capital and the same rate of exploitation, S/V.

Nevertheless, the rates of profit in various lines of industry with different organic compositions of capital must also be equalized in the market. If, in the long run, rates of profit differed in different industries, firms would leave low-profit industries and move into high-profit industries. This would be so regardless of the organic composition of capital in each industry.

Marx provides the following example to show "how the average rate of profit is formed from different organic compositions of capital and how the values of commodities are transformed into their prices."

Let us assume that the sum of constant plus variable capital in five industries equals 100, with different organic compositions of capital in each (see table 9.1 on page 90). Next assume a 100 percent rate of surplus value (rate of exploitation). In that case, surplus value in each case will equal variable capital for each industry. The rate of profit $S/(C + V)$, column 5 in the table, differs for each of the five industries. Industry I is 20 percent, II is 30 percent, III is 40 percent, IV is 15 percent, and V is 5 percent.

The differences in the rates of profit are due to the differences in original capital. (For this exercise only, the Cs in column 2 will be designated as C' in order to represent capital investment, not used-up capital.) In column 2, for example, industry I has 80 C' and 20 V, II has 70 C' and 30 V. Used-up capital C (not C', table 9.1, column 6) depends on the nature of capital equipment, its durability, an1 so on. Thus, used-up C is selected arbitrarily by Marx for purposes of example only.

The values of capital used up *(C* in table 9.1, column 6) are 50, 51, 51, 40, and 10. The values of commodities shown on table 9.1, column 7, are constructed by replacing the original C's in column 2 with used-up capitals. This provides the values of commodities for each industry (column 7). I is 90; II, 111; III, 131; and so forth.

Finally, in table 9.1, is the cost-price of a commodity in each industry. Cost-price includes only variable capital (*V* from column 2) plus used-up capital. Surplus value is not a part of the cost of production. The value of commodities represents the socially necessary labor time used to produce a unit of a product in each of the five industries.

At the bottom of table 9.1, capitals are added together and divided by five to give the average original C' and V for all the industries taken together. The sum of C's, 390, divided by 5, is 78. The sum of Vs, 110, divided by 5, is 22. At the bottom of the surplus-value column is the average surplus value or profit for the entire economy. Because of the simplifying assumption that $S = V$, wages are the same as profits. Marx wants to show that after competition has done its work to shift investment from the low-profit industries to the high (lowering the profit of the high and increasing the profit of the low), the average rate of profit for all industries after competition is 22 percent.

Table 9.2 is easier to interpret. The first five columns are similar to columns in table 9.1. Thus far, nothing new. But, column 6 labeled "Commodities —Price of," is new. It represents the $C + V + S$ where the individual rates of profit for each industry prior to competition are replaced by 22, the average for all industries taken together. The next-to-the-last column in table 9.2 shows the problem with the labor theory of value that Marx himself saw. Cost-price of commodities (column 5) will always differ from the value of commodities (column 4) once competition has equalized rates of profit in all industries. The last column of table 9.2 shows the deviation of price from value (column 6 minus column 4). The pluses and minuses always cancel out, but the point is that the prices will always deviate from values except when all used-up Cs in all industries happen to be equal—an unlikely situation given the necessary differences in compositions of capital.

Since values and prices always differ, it raises the question of what Marx is talking about when he says that the value of a commodity is equal to the socially necessary labor time embodied in it. To answer in Marx's own words: "This always amounts in the end to saying that one commodity receives too

TABLE 9.1

Industry	Compositions of Capital	Rate of Surplus Value S/V (%)	Surplus Value S	Rate of Profit $S/(C+V)$ (%)	Used-up Capital C	Value of Commodities $C+V+S$	Cost-Price of $C+V$
1	2	3	4	5	6	7	8
I	80C' + 20V	100	20	20	50	90	70
II	70C' + 30V	100	30	30	51	111	81
III	60C' + 40V	100	40	40	51	131	91
IV	85C' + 15V	100	15	15	40	70	55
V	95C' + 5V	100	5	5	10	20	15
TOTAL	390C' + 110V	110	110				
AVERAGE	78C' + 22V	22	22				

Source: *Capital*, 3:185.

little of the surplus value while another receives too much, so that the deviations from the value shown by the prices of production mutually compensate one another. In short, under capitalist production, the general law of value enforces itself merely as the prevailing tendency, in a very complicated and appropriate manner, as a never ascertainable average of ceaseless fluctuations."[14]

A little later in *Capital*, Marx adds that if the commodities are sold at their cost-price value, there are different rates of profit in each industry according to the different organic compositions of capital invested in them. Nevertheless, he concludes, the competitive process under capitalism does not allow such differences to persist.

Market Prices and Market Values

Market prices and market values (prices or costs of the production of commodities) will continue to differ. The value of the commodity is determined by labor time spent on it in only a "vague and meaningless form." Nevertheless, the law of values dominates market prices. For commodities to exchange with one another at their values, there must be (1) an established market, (2) large quantities exchanged, and (3) no monopoly. These values, so established, are only the average around which prices fluctuate—some commodities selling above and some below value. Despite the fact that prices fluctuate on a day-to-day basis, market prices cannot be understood without reference to the labor theory of value on which demand-supply relations rest. And then, Marx notes: "Only in this vague and meaningless form are we still reminded of the fact that the value of commodities is determined by the labor contained in them."[15]

Marx insists, nevertheless, that values lie behind prices, although they may not be identical. "Whatever may be the way in which the prices of the various commodities are first fixed or mutually regulated, the law of value [cost price of commodities] always dominates their movements. If the labor time required for the production of the commodities is reduced, prices fall; if it is increased, prices rise, other circumstances remaining the same."[16]

And further, Marx declares: "The assumption that the commodities of the various spheres of production are sold at their value implies, of course, only that their value is the center of gravity around which prices fluctuate."[17] Market prices may be higher or lower than the costs of production of commodities according to market conditions. But even market prices cannot depart very far from the prices of production. The law of value dominates the movement of prices because a reduction in labor time tends to lower the center of gravity around which prices fluctuate, whereas an increase in necessary labor time raises it.

TABLE 9.2

Industry	Compositions of Capital	Surplus Value	Commodities Value of	Commodities Cost-Price of	Commodities Price of	Rate of Profit (%)	Deviation of Price from Value
1	2	3	4	5	6	7	8
I	80C' + 20V	20	90	70	92	22	+ 2
II	70C' + 30V	30	111	81	103	22	− 8
III	60C' + 40V	40	131	91	113	22	−18
IV	85C' + 15V	15	70	55	77	22	+ 7
V	95C' + 5V	5	20	15	37	22	+17

SOURCE: See table 9.1.

Competition not only equalizes the rate of profit but also determines average prices. Neither can profits be increased at the expense of labor income nor can real (price adjusted) income be influenced by price changes. Real wages cannot fall below the level of subsistence. Wages can rise above subsistence when profits rise due to a reduction in the costs of production. A rise or fall in the prices of production can occur only when there is an increase or decrease in the socially necessary labor time used to produce commodities. What Marx is saying is that the value of commodities (column 4 in table 9.2), not simply market prices, determines what actually happens in a capitalist economy. "As a general law," he says, "as a principle regulating the fluctuations [of prices] it follows that the law of value regulates the prices of production."[18]

Competition among industries brings about equal rates of profit for each of them. "This last process requires a higher development of capitalist production than the previous process."[19]

Marx insists once more that absolutely nothing can be explained by the relation of supply and demand unless the basis on which the relation rests has first been ascertained. Thus for Marx there are three prices to be considered: cost-prices or value prior to competition, prices of production after competition, and, finally, market prices that fluctuate due to supply and demand, which may be above or below the prices or values of production.

Summary

Marx uses the word "value" to refer to the socially necessary labor time embodied in a commodity. Table 9.2 (column 4) illustrates Marx's usage. The value of a commodity is the sum of $C + V + S$ before competition equalizes the rates of profit among industries. After competition, "value" becomes "price." Table 9.2 (column 6) differs from "value." The reason for this difference is that S (surplus value), which before competition differed from industry to industry, is now uniform because competition equalizes the rate of profit in every industry. (In Marx's illustration in table 9.2, column 7, S is equal to 22 for *every* industry.) Thus the sum of $C + V + S$ in column 6 is not the same as that in column 4. Already, Marx provides reason for market prices to vary from their values.

Yet the story is not concluded. Marx declares that *actual* market prices, those that face the consumer, will differ from the market prices illustrated in his example because of the forces of demand and supply. Contemporary economists remain unimpressed with Marx's demonstration. They are not concerned with values in the Marxist sense because they are unobservable. For contemporary economics, asking what the "real" value of a commodity is, is an exercise in metaphysics, not economics. Contemporary economists wish to understand how observed market prices are formed.

Contemporary economists are also interested, as were Marx and Ricardo, in where, in the absence of random and temporary pressures, prices would come to rest in equilibrium. Marx insists that the question of what determines equilibrium prices in the long run cannot be answered without knowing the "value" of a commodity—the socially necessary labor time content of it. Furthermore, understanding that underlying the price of any commodity is the socially necessary labor time used to produce it—whether looking at prices that obtain after competition or their temporary market prices (those observed) —helps illuminate the dynamics of capitalism.

Marx's successors have tried to connect observed prices with "values" as determined by the labor theory of value. To do so, they have shown how "values" can be transformed into prices. A vast literature on "the transformation problem" has developed to show that a reconciliation of market prices and values is possible.

When Marx accepts the classical doctrine that profits, through competition, tend to equality throughout the economy, and that there will be a long-term tendency for the rate of profit within the economy to decline, his understanding of the capitalist economy coincides with more orthodox views of how the economy works. But, his reasons for concluding that profits fall in the long run differ from those of such classical economists as David Ricardo.

Marx asserts, but provides no proof, that profit will decline in the long run. The expression of the determinants of the rate of profit, $S/(C + V)$, cannot show that S inevitably rises less than C rises when C is replacing V, living labor input. This ambiguity has been the subject of discussion by Marx's critics and supporters.

If there are "tendencies" that counteract the law of the eventually declining rate of profit, how long may those tendencies continue before being overwhelmed by the underlying forces that signal permanent and irreversible decline? Without a theory that argues that counteracting tendencies are temporary and ephemeral, or one that can distinguish between events that only represent tendencies and those that are decisive, the observer can never predict that a measured decline in the rate of profit, even over an extensive period, is evidence that a fatal decline in the rate of profits is at hand.

The view that the rate of profit must decline is essential to the Marxist System. According to Marx, capitalism grows through the reinvestment of profits. Without surplus value, profits dry up. Without profits, capitalism dies. In chapter 10 we see how the logic of Marx's system leads to the death of capitalism and its replacement by socialism.

CHAPTER 10

CAPITALISM:
CRISES AND BREAKDOWN

In the Marxist System, capitalists perform the social function of accumulating capital. It is necessary to capitalism that the capitalist continually attempt to extend that capital. The capitalist is coerced by external forces to accumulate. Capitalism is full of contradictions, some causing temporary crises that are more or less serious. But a fundamental cause of eventual breakdown is due at least in part to the inherent inability of capitalism to distribute income widely enough to purchase the ever-growing output of a very productive economic system, and more certainly due to the tendency for profits to fall toward zero. First, I discuss the long-run course of the decline of capitalism. Second, in the section entitled "Crises," I discuss the tendency of a capitalist economy to be unstable and subject to business cycles.

Capitalism and Accumulation

The capitalist accumulates for his own "transitory existence," not for the enjoyment or use of production but for the exchange value and for purposes of increasing his accumulation. "Fanatically bent on making value expand itself, he ruthlessly forces the human race to produce for production's sake; he thus forces the development of the productive powers of society, and creates those material conditions, which alone can form the real basis of a higher form of society, a society in which the full and free development of every individual forms the ruling principle."[1]

The capitalist is impelled by a social mechanism of which "he is but one of the wheels." The process of capitalist development makes it constantly necessary to keep increasing the amount of capital laid out in a given industrial undertaking. The laws of capitalist development are felt by each capitalist as "external coercive laws." To preserve his capital he must constantly extend it. The only way he can extend it is by progressive accumulation. "To accumulate, is to conquer the world of social wealth, to increase the mass of human beings exploited by him, and thus extend both the direct and indirect sway of the capitalist."[2]

Each capitalist is avaricious, has a strong urge to get rich. But the progress of capitalist production "not only creates a world of delights" but lays open in speculation and the credit system "a thousand sources of sudden enrichment." When sources of credit become a business necessity, "luxury enters into capital's expenses of representation." The capitalist gets rich, not like the miser by personal labor and restricted consumption, but "as he squeezes out the labor power of others and enforces on the laborer abstinences from all life's enjoyments."[3]

The Reserve Army of the Unemployed

In the process of capitalist accumulation, a shortage of labor may develop, wages will increase, and an improvement in the condition of the working class may occur. Increasing wages will not bring forth an increase in the numbers of the working class. Here Marx does not accept Malthus's assumption about the connection between real wages and population growth. Marx believes Malthus's theory—population will increase as an automatic function of above-subsistence wages—to be a libel on the human race. Humans behave more rationally than Malthus believes.

The process of accumulation ultimately reduces the demand for labor as machinery replaces living capital. In the process of capital accumulation, workers are continually replaced by machinery, according to Marx. The decline in the employment of living labor is relative. The absolute numbers of employed may increase, but their numbers will decline relative to total capital. In the process of accumulation there are "violent" fluctuations in employment. Surplus population is created as the ratio of constant to variable capital grows. The labor supply grows to meet the increased demand for labor, "only to be dismissed as the organic composition of capital increases." As a result an "ever-growing industrial reserve army of unemployed develops, which stands ready to meet the next wave of expansion of industries." The economic function of overpopulation is to provide for the periodic and sudden expansion of industry.

Marx's research leads him to the conclusion that a capitalist economy endures a ten-year business cycle that depends on the constant formation of capital, the greater or lesser absorption of unemployed labor, and again the formation of a reserve army. Bourgeois economists, according to Marx, see business cycles as a problem related to the expansion and contraction of credit. But in doing so, they see only a symptom of the real problem, which is the nature of capitalist accumulation.

Bourgeois economists blame falling wages on population increases. Marx disagrees. The course of a business cycle (ten years) is too short to account for the eighteen-year period it takes to achieve significant population increases. Capitalists blame the proletariat for its own unemployment. The truth is that capitalism simply cannot absorb a growing labor force.

Laborers try to protect themselves from the fluctuations of business cycles by forming trade unions. As soon as the workforce increases during a period of expansion, laborers foresee the danger of a future increase in the reserve army of the unemployed during the next recession. They thus form trade unions to head off wage cuts due to the expected competition from excess workers. But when they organize, "capitalists invoke the sacred law of supply and demand," and utilize the state to interfere forcibly with trade union activity. Marx claims that low wages are a consequence of capitalist modes of production, not Lassalle's "iron law of wages" or Malthusian population theory. If Malthus's and Lassalle's laws were natural laws, changing the social relations of production could not change them.

Marx argues that the wage-labor system can be abolished only when capitalism disappears. His attack on Lassalle's "iron law of wages," which is founded on Malthusian population theory, makes the critical point. Marx describes the "iron law" thus:

"The iron economic law, which under present-day conditions under the role of the supply and demand for labor determines wages, is this: that the average wage always remains reduced to the necessary basis of subsistence that . . . *is requisite for existence and propagation.*"

Lassalle speaks of abolishing "the wage system." Marx says he should speak of abolishing the system of wage labor, together with the "iron law of wages." "If I abolish wage labor, then naturally I abolish its laws also, whether they are iron or sponge." He comments that Lassalle's attack on wage labor is really an attack on the "iron law."

But if Lassalle's "iron law" is based on Malthusian population theory, and if Malthus is correct, "I cannot abolish the law even if I abolish wage labor a hundred times over, because the law then governs not only the system of wage labor but every social system."[4] If the law is based on natural law and every increase in living standard is followed by an increase in population, as conservative economists had argued for fifty years, says Marx, socialism cannot abolish poverty but can only impoverish the entire society.

Monopoly Capitalism, the Last Stage of Capitalism

The process of capitalist accumulation, once begun, becomes the means for further accumulation. At first, the number of capitalists tends to increase largely as a result of the division of capital among family members. Wealth tends to grow on itself and become concentrated in the hands of individual capitalists.

The concentration of capital in fewer hands arises from two factors: (1) the amount of social wealth available for concentration increases, and (2) competition among capitalists increases as well. Not only do competition and the advantages of scale concentrate capital, but amalgamation through mergers concentrates capital in the hands of individuals. At this point monopoly capitalism is in the last stage in its development.

One consequence of concentration is that fewer and fewer laborers are required to work the capital. The growth of monopoly capitalists reduces the demand for labor. In the stage of monopoly, crises of capitalism arise from the misery, oppression, degradation, and slavery of laborers. They revolt. The death knell of capitalist private property tolls and the expropriators are themselves expropriated by a desperate working class whose eyes have been opened to their true condition.

Capitalism develops this way: With competition, the increase in the minimum capital required for the successful operation of an independent industrial establishment keeps pace with the increase in productivity. As new and more expensive equipment comes into production, it displaces the older equipment of smaller capitalists. Smaller capitalists can survive only during the early stages of mechanical inventions. On the other hand, large enterprises such as railroads, which have very high constant to variable capital ratios, yield surplus value in the form of interest (interest and rents, as well as profits, are deductions from surplus value). Large masses of capital can earn very little surplus value because they employ so few living laborers.

As time passes, increases in capital accumulation require less labor. Surplus value declines when the proportion of variable to constant capital becomes smaller and smaller. In boom times, however, both old and new methods of production exist side by side, proving that the numbers of employees at work may be expanding while both old and new methods of production proceed. Thus the fall in the rate of profit may be slower than the accumulation of capital.

The number of laborers at work may increase temporarily in spite of the relative decrease in variable capital compared with constant capital. Changes in capital composition do not take place uniformly in all lines of production, although in agriculture living labor may be declining absolutely. There may be fluctuations in the absolute number of living laborers at work at particular times. Hidden in these fluctuations is the trend toward decline in the employment of living labor. Should employment decline all at once, there would be revolution.

The inability to employ living labor continuously shows that capitalism is not "an absolute form for the development of productive powers and the creation of wealth."[5] Capitalism is in conflict with itself. Capitalists expand production and employ labor for the purpose of creating surplus value for themselves. The replacement of workers with machinery is socially desirable in that it decreases the amount of labor expended on necessary work. But since under capitalism the replacement of workers with machinery dries up the source of investment funds (surplus value), social ills are exacerbated. The long-run purpose of capital accumulation—the creation of social wealth—comes into conflict with capitalism's need to expand continuously through the reinvestment of profits. Yet because reinvestment takes the form of replacing living labor with capital equipment, both the capitalists' interests and those of the larger society are frustrated.[6] The contradiction leads to an irreconcilable crash "which implies the dissolution of these relations."[7]

The death rattle of capitalism is described in a variety of ways. Marx's description found in *Capital* is worth reading in its entirety.

"As soon as this process of transformation has sufficiently decomposed the old society from top to bottom, as soon as the laborers are turned into proletarians, their means of labor into capital, as soon as the capitalist mode of production stands on its own feet, then the further socialization of labor and further transformation of the land and other means of production into socially exploited and, therefore, common means of production, as well as the further expropriation of private proprietors, takes a new form. That which is now to be expropriated is no longer the laborer working for himself, but the capitalist exploiting many laborers. This expropriation is accomplished by the action of immanent laws of capitalistic production itself, by the centralization of capital.

"One capitalist always kills many. Hand in hand with this centralization, or this expropriation of many capitalists by few, develop, on an ever extending scale, the cooperative form of the labor-process, the conscious technical application of science, the methodical cultivation of the soil, the transformation of the instruments of labor into instruments of labor only usable in common, the economizing of all means of production by their use as the means of production of combined, socialized labor, the entanglement of all peoples in the net of the world-market, and thus, the international character of the capitalistic regime.

"Along with the constantly diminishing number of the magnates of capital, who usurp and monopolize all advantages of this process of transformation, grows the mass of misery, oppression, slavery, degradation, exploitation; but with this too grows the revolt of the working-class, a class always increasing in numbers, and disciplined, united, organized by the very mechanism of the process of capitalist production itself. The monopoly of capital becomes a fetter upon the mode of production, which has sprung up and flourished along with, and under it. Centralization of the means of production and socialization of labor at least reach a point where they become incompatible with their capitalist integument [shell]. This integument is burst asunder. The knell of capitalist private property sounds. The expropriators are expropriated."[8]

Marx shows that during the course of capitalist development there are business fluctuations (cycles). While not in themselves fatal to capitalism, they create economic chaos. As the capitalist economy declines over time, business cycles become more severe and intractable. What are the causes of these cycles? Here are some of Marx's analyses.

Crises

DEFICIENCY IN DEMAND

The creation of surplus value does not in itself assure profit; sale of the goods on the market is necessary. But the consumer must have purchasing power to buy what is produced. The sale of product is limited by the consuming power of the public. But after each round of accumulation, the consuming power of the public falls further.

This contradiction is inherent in capitalism. Periodically, overproduction (or underconsumption) of the necessities of life reduces surplus value, indicating that accumulation cannot go on forever without causing explosions. What is occurring is not true overproduction, but overproduction in its capitalist form. Consumption is curtailed by the very forces that realize value. There are two separate acts: the one, extracting surplus value in the act of production; the other, realizing that surplus value in the sale price of the product. The contradiction is manifest.

While the inability to sell a commodity may appear to be a result of too much production, this is not the case. It is the development of productive power that creates the falling rate of profit, "a law which turns into an antagonism of this mode of production at a certain point and requires for its defeat periodical crises."[9]

Another way of putting Marx's proposition is that the expansion or contraction of production is determined by the capitalists' ability to extract surplus value. The expansion and contraction of production are driven by the expectation that profits will not fall below a certain minimum. Investment, "instead of being determined by the relation of production to social wants, to the wants of socially developed human beings," depends on the needs of capitalists for profits.[10] A deficiency in demand develops when there are not enough paid workers to purchase the ever-increasing volume of output that the economy is capable of producing.

WAGES

Deficiency in demand cannot be counteracted simply by raising wages. If the solvency of consumers were the entire problem, simply raising wages for working people would solve it. But high wages would cut into surplus value, the source of profits. Yet all crises are preceded by a period of rising wages. Rising wages help squeeze capitalist profits during the boom of an economy and thus contribute to, rather than avert, the crisis. In the long run, the greater the proportion of income that goes to workers' wages, the lower the capitalists' profits.

INTERNAL CONTRADICTIONS

A fall in the rate of profit hastens accumulation, and accumulation hastens the fall in the rate of profit. A fall in the rate of profit hastens the concentration of wealth in the hands of a few capitalists. New accumulation is checked by the fall in the rate of profit and threatens capitalist development by bringing about speculations, crises, and surplus capital and population. Capitalism is caught in a vicious circle.

The history of capitalism is a history of crises. Economic crises are among the manifestations of capitalism's internal contradictions. The concentration of capital in a few hands also brings crises. Large firms with small rates of profit can accumulate faster than small firms with high profit rates. Small firms are driven to adventurous channels such as speculation, fraudulent credit, fraudulent stocks, and crises. These maneuvers by capitalists are not effective enough to enable them to survive the decline in the rate of profit.

When the output from existing capital cannot be sold on the market, some proportion of capital must remain idle. Since net profit is calculated on both productive and idle capital, it is to the advantage of the capitalist—for the purpose of excluding competition—to keep new capital idle in order to protect the value of existing capital. A progressive struggle among capitalists is likely to ensue in order to minimize losses within their social class. But in such a situation the capitalist class as a whole loses. Idle capital results in the economic crises that are among the manifestations of capitalism's internal contradictions.

At the end of each crisis, equilibrium is restored by the "slaughtering of the values of capital," resulting in a sharp decline in the value of fixed capital.

Violent and acute crises force sudden depreciation, stagnation, and the collapse of the process of reproduction. Wages fall as unemployment restores surplus value. Accumulation commences once again, producing goods more cheaply since prices have already fallen. Depreciation has reduced the value of constant capital relative to variable, and the cycle continues to run its course.

SAY'S LAW, MONETARY CRISIS, AND DISPROPORTIONS IN PRODUCTION

Marx is critical of the view of classical economists that business cycles are impossible in a market economy. Say's law is a case in point. According to J.B. Say, the French classical economist, there can be no general overproduction because products exchange against products: "No man produces but with a view to consume or sell, and he never sells but with an intention to purchase some other commodity which may be immediately useful to him, or which may contribute to future production." Marx demurs, making the central point that what may be true in a barter economy may not be true in a money economy. In the latter, production must be sold for money, and money must be borrowed from banks and reinvested. Unless both occur, stagnation will follow.

In reproduction, that is, in replacing used-up capital with new, capitalists insist that the new capital earn the same rate of profit as the capital being replaced. If, for whatever reasons, market prices fall below the costs of production, the reproduction of capital will be considerably curtailed. And without the prospect of profit, new investment will not be undertaken. Money will lie idle. Using idle funds to purchase gold or simply maintaining unused credit at the bank will cause financial losses to firms and stagnation in the economy.

Marx catalogues what can go wrong in a money economy. Economic stagnation can occur for a variety of reasons. If, for example, grain became expensive and could not be sold at profitable prices or if there were a shortage of materials with which to reproduce capital equipment, stagnation could occur. A stagnant economy is marked by unsold goods on the market and unemployed capital in the form of idle money in banks.

Also, if a surplus of money capital accumulates so rapidly that its retransformation into the means of production (capital equipment) cannot keep pace, there will be a rise in the price of all relevant commodities (due to a shortage of them). At the same time, the accumulation of money in the bank will cause the rate of interest to fall rapidly. Cheap money will lead to risky, speculative ventures. Failure to reproduce capital (new investment) decreases the demand for variable capital (for labor), wages will fall and unemployment rise, triggering a new fall in prices.

Crises are not immediately self-correcting or self-limiting. All kinds of things can happen during a crisis. Catastrophes may develop; new crises may occur, "which cannot in any way be got rid of by the pitiful claptrap [Say's law] that products exchange against products."

Marx complains that some economists deny the possibility of an overabundance of commodities while affirming the possibility of an overproduction of capital. Others attempt to deny the unpleasant truth that capitalists compete with one another not only as sellers of goods but as owners of capital.

But an overabundance of capital is not the same as an overabundance of money, since money and capital are different kinds of commodities. The particular relationship of overproduction of both capital and commodities is one that holds in a capitalist economy but in no other. The reason for this is that the overproduction of commodities and capital occurs in the absence of planning, so capital may be created without foreknowledge of whether the commodities produced with them are those wanted by the public.

The belief, derived from Say's law of markets, that every purchase is a sale, is refuted by the occurrence of crises. In a money economy, often the only way that all produced goods can be sold is for capitalists to sharply reduce commodity prices. How can crises be denied, as Say's law clearly denies them? Marx's answer to that question is that economists see money only as a medium of exchange, whereas money is essentially an independent form of commodity. Monetary phenomena make crises possible, they do not cause crises. In premarket societies, where there is no price system, crises are unknown.

The characteristic use of money in capitalism takes two forms. First, a commodity in its form of use value is transformed into money (c to m)—that is, is sold for money. Second, a purchase is made (m to c). The possibility of crisis comes about when sales are separated from purchases. In a barter economy the problem would not exist. The possibility of crisis in another form arises out of money as a means of payment (m to c).

Money in the process of reproduction of capital must pass through the c–m–c process, the metamorphosis of the commodity. In this process crises may arise because of the separation of purchase and sale. The first metamorphosis consists of turning capital into money; the second, of turning money into capital.

Some capitals are in the process of turning themselves into money, and others are going from money to capital. This uncoordinated movement of capital goods and commodities into money and money into capital goods is made possible by the division of labor and is often accidental. Thus the exchange economy, with its complex division of labor, provides the environment in which crises may develop.

Marx provides an example of how money as a means of payment can create the possibility of a crisis. He cites the manufacturing of cloth, wherein each participant—the growers, spinners, weavers, and others—are financed by the advance of credit based on the expected receipts from final sales to consumers. Given a default at any point in the network of credit, the chain of purchase and sale is broken, and there is the possibility of an ensuing crisis.

Contemporary economists, says Marx, are unable to reason crises out of existence. They believed that crises were simply caused by monetary phenomena and were accidental. What they failed to perceive was that monetary crises were only the manifest forms in which crises appear and were not the fundamental causes of the breakdown of capitalism.

EXPANSION OF PRODUCTION AND EXPANSION
IN THE MARKET AS CAUSES OF CRISES

In discussing the expansion of production in relation to the expansion of the market, Marx explains that crises arise when the market as a whole expands more slowly than productive capacity.

"Overproduction" is a misleading word if one means that more products are produced than there is need for. Only in capitalist modes of production does overproduction occur. In reality, there is always underproduction in terms of the needs of people. The limit of production is capitalist profit. It is impossible, Marx says, for bourgeois economists to admit that the bourgeois mode of production creates its own barrier to further production.

Marx claims that "bourgeois" economists argue as follows: There is no universal overproduction (an equal amount of overproduction everywhere) because equal overproduction would be the same as proportional overproduction, which is simply a greater than usual production in all spheres.

If iron is overproduced, this thinking goes, it cannot be said that coal is overproduced as well, because to overproduce iron involves a similar overproduction of coal. One cannot speak of overproduction of raw materials that enter into the production of goods that have been overproduced. Yet it is possible, even probable, that coal could be overproduced, that is, produced beyond the needs of the iron industry, because the production schedule of coal is determined by the rate by which all coal-using industries are expanding rather than by the immediate demand for coal. The calculation of coal requirements may be overshot. It is therefore nonsense to say that overproduction in the coal industry is due to underproduction elsewhere.

Even when bourgeois economists admit the possibility of overproduction in each particular branch of production, Marx notes, they maintain that what prevents a general glut is that commodities are exchanged for other commodities rather than for money. They deny that commodities can remain unsold because they believe that an increase in production automatically creates a market for all output. The whole bourgeois position thus rests on the assumption of a moneyless economy. In fact, says Marx, the separation of production from sale in a market economy implies the possibility of unsold commodities.

For example, if newly produced capital goods are to be sold, their prices must not be higher than those of existing goods. And this may not be the case. Strong expansion in the production of capital goods may result in higher demand for, and higher prices of, the raw materials that enter into their production. Or prices of raw materials may rise due to scarcity—in the case, for example, of agricultural products when harvests are poor. High costs of capital goods unaccompanied by a high demand for the commodities they produce may result in a crisis of overproduction.

Summary

In the Marxist System, crises of various kinds ultimately accumulate; for example, disproportions in production among different branches of production, monetary crises, overproduction, underconsumption, the development of monopolies out of competitive firms, a deficiency in demand because of low wages and unemployment, and a reserve army of unemployed. And always, the downward trend in profits, resulting from the gradual replacement of labor by capital equipment, continues to sap the vitality of capitalism by draining away the living labor that is its life's blood until accumulation becomes impossible. Without the ability to accumulate capital, the role of capitalism disappears and the institutions that defend it become redundant. Bereft of its rationale, with the loss of support of the capitalist class (most of which has been forced into the ranks of the proletariat), capitalism then self-destructs.

Modern economists have admired Marx's pioneering work on business cycles, his discussion of the role of money in economic crises, his recognition that individuals may wish to hold money as cash rather than spend it on production or consumption. And Marx makes clear his belief that much of the disproportions of wealth under capitalism is the result of a lack of "planning," a fault he sees as inherent in capitalism.

Some of Marx's observations about how a capitalist economy actually operates are subject to empirical tests: Are investments in new capital always labor saving, inevitably creating unemployment? His other observations are theoretical, deductions from prior assumptions. Because profit is derived only from living labor (an assumption), profits must fall as capital replaces labor in the process of production (a deduced consequence).

Chapter 11 completes the review of the Marxist System with a consideration of his discussion of the downfall of capitalism and its culture and its replacement with socialism and communism.

Appendix: Capitalist Reproduction

"Simple reproduction" is the term Marx uses to describe what in elementary economics textbooks is referred to as the circular flow of production. It is a schematic representation of the process by which income is continuously circulated from consumption to production and from production back to consumption in an endless flow, without increase or diminution of production or consumption. In simple reproduction, there is no capital accumulation and therefore no growth in the productive potential of the economy. Following the time-honored method of exposition in economics, Marx begins his analysis with the simplest model. He explains simple reproduction.

Capitalism is, however, quintessentially a system for the accumulation of capital. To explain capital accumulation, or "extended reproduction," Marx complicates his model of simple reproduction. His incomplete remarks about simple and extended reproduction appear in *Capital,* volume 2.

Marx posits two producing sectors, one that produces consumer goods and one that produces capital goods. In simple reproduction, the only function of the capital goods sector is to replace equipment used in the production of consumer goods and to replace capital goods worn out in its own sector. In simple reproduction, all production is for consumption, and individuals in their capacity as consumers spend all the income they earn in their capacity as producers so as to enable both sectors to be fully financed. This exhausts their income as consumers and provides sufficient finance for both sectors to continue production, neither diminished nor augmented. Among classical economists, such a changeless flow defines a "stationary state," a situation that can continue indefinitely if there is no added or "net" investment.

Marx puts it this way: "The annual product includes those portions of the social product which reproduce capital, the social reproduction, as well as those which go to the fund for consumption, which are consumed by capitalists and laborers, in other words, productive and individual consumption."[11] From this distinction Marx intended to go forward to explain the concept of capital accumulation, "net investment." Unfortunately, he did not get around to completing his discussion of what he called "accumulation on an expanded scale."

Marx describes the process of circular flow of real output and money income by positing two separate departments. Department I consists of the annual output of the capital goods industry that must produce the capital for its own continuance over time as well as the capital for the replacement of the used-up capital of Department II. Department II is the consumer goods department, which must not only provide consumption goods for its own producers but also provide for the worker and capitalist consumption of Department I.

This is his scheme:

Department I

$$4000C_1 + 1000V_1 + 1000S_1 = 6000 \text{ Value of Capital Goods}$$

Department II

$$2000C_2 + 500V_2 + 500S_2 = 3000 \text{ Value of Consumer Goods}$$

To keep the economy stationary, Department I must provide itself and Department II with replacements for used up capital $C_2 + C_1$, while Department II must provide consumer goods for both departments. That is, Department II provides $(V_1 + V_2) + (S_1 + S_2)$. The output of both departments is used up in providing for each other. There is no capital accumulation and therefore no economic growth. The exposition works out this way:

Department II

$$2000C_2 + 500V_2 + 500S_2 = (1000V_1 + 500V_2) + (1000S_1 + 500S_2)$$

When the S_2 and V_2 are deducted from both sides, there remains: $V_1 + S_1 = C_2$. Department II has brought consumer goods to the capital goods sector.

Department I

$$4000C_1 + 1000V_1 + 1000S_1 = 4000C_1 + 2000C_2$$

When C_1 is deducted from both sides, there remains: $V_1 + S_1 = C_2$. Department I has been repaid for its contribution of consumer goods to Department II by the receipt of replacement capital from Department I.

Having shown the process of circular flow without capital accumulation, Marx proceeds to demonstrate the process of "Accumulation and Reproduction" that is so necessary to economic growth. We have seen that in both Departments I and II, $C_2 = V_1 + S_1$. The first step in capital accumulation is to hold as "hoards" of money the depreciation (C) in both departments. Marx sees money as a store of value, used in a market economy to facilitate the purchase of commodities at different points in time. And he sees the source of investment funds as capitalist savings (nonconsumption) out of profits (surplus value).[12]

In simple reproduction, $C_2 = V_1 + S_1$. For capital to accumulate, the sum of S and V must exceed C. Marx provides an example below:

Department I
$$4000C_1 + 1000V_1 + 1000S_1 = 6000$$

Department II
$$1500C_2 + 376V_2 + 376S_2 = 2252$$

Here the sum of $V_1 + S_1 = 2000$, which is greater than the $1500C_2$ by the amount of $500S_1$ of Department I. Department I can purchase 1500 C_2 from Department II and have $500S_1$ left over for investment in itself. Assuming that Department I does invest its $500S_1$ in itself, and assuming, as Marx does, that a department can transfer resources *internally* among capitalists in the department without money payment (as if the department were one large firm), there is no problem of paying for resources invested within a department. But Department II also has some surplus resources, amounting to $376S_2$. If we assume that Department II will be satisfied to invest half, or $188S_2$, in itself, there remains the $188S_2$ for Department I to use. How is Department I to pay for the resources it wishes to purchase from Department II? Marx sees the problem of shifting the $188S_2$ (one-half of the S_2 generated in Department II) from the consumer goods sector to the capital goods sector, Department I. Here we have a one-sided purchase from Department II, that is, a purchase without a sale of goods to Department II. The $188S_2$ must be paid for from "hoards," but there are no "hoards" in Department I to shift to II.

Marx explores some unacceptable solutions to the financing problem. If wages *(V)* are above subsistence, as they may sometimes be, wages can be reduced by a variety of schemes to levels even below the value of a worker's labor power. The only other source of funds, the capitalists' own funds, Marx suggests, partly in jest, can be raised by cheating and robbing one another. Marx also rejects "falsification" (presumably inflation) of the currency. These options are unacceptable to Marx because they do violence to his basic theory that capitalism's problems do not derive from capitalist manipulation but from its inner dynamics. Marx does not completely answer the question of where the money comes from, however, when he explains that Department II, just as in the case of Department I, can finance itself by shifting resources, moneylessly, *within* the department. Where each department gets the money to purchase *from each other* is basically left unanswered. Volume 2 of *Capital* ends abruptly and inconclusively at that point.

However satisfactorily the financing problem is solved, Marx's theory of capital accumulation and growth of the national income is very close to that of modern models of economic growth in which capital accumulation and national income grow at a steady rate (constant percentage). If capitalists continuously set aside the same percentage of surplus value and variable capital for the purpose of reinvestment, the rates of growth of profit, of investment, and of national income will also be the same. For example, assume 50 percent of S is reinvested always in new constant capital. Assume 12.5 percent of S is invested always in necessary variable capital. If we postulate the rate of surplus value ($S/V = 100$ percent), then 12.5 percent of V creates 12.5 percent of S at a constant rate. The source of the surplus value is living labor (V). The continued growth of surplus value, in turn, assures a continuous source of funds for capital accumulation and national income *at a constant rate*. One must remember that for Marx, S declines as a proportion of national income because constant capital increases over time. Therefore, Marx does not expect the rate of growth of national income to remain constant. It falls in the long run along with the decline in the rate of profit.

COMMUNISM

My review of the Marxist System is completed. It is a system that elaborates on the ways in which the economy and civilization of capitalism grow out of earlier systems. Like its predecessors, the system of capitalism will complete its historically necessary mission and then disappear. For the process, it creates all of the tools necessary for humans to conquer nature and turn it to human purposes. But the civilization created by capitalism, more than any other system, is devastating to the human spirit. Indeed, the enormity of the misery of the proletariat is the condition predating its redemption in communism. We are now ready to see how Marx describes the death throes of capitalism and the birth of communism.

For Marx, communism is not a clearly defined condition, as is capitalism. His attempts at definition constitute an incomplete statement about social and interpersonal relations as they would exist in a communist structure. Why no blueprint for the society yet to be born? To provide one would violate Marx's sense of the historical nature of society. Writing blueprints for societies yet to come would be simply a utopian construct of the imagination, no more valid than the fantasy world of an Owen or a Fourier, which he condemns.

However, Marx provides clues to the nature of his vision in the form of generalizations about the world of communism, wherein he shows how the transition from a dying capitalism will occur and what some of the human and social relations will of necessity look like under a new communist order.

In the communist world to come, for instance, there will be no classes and consequently no antagonism between people. Not only will economics disappear in a world without scarce resources, but all power relationships will disappear. Whatever compulsion to produce that exists will come from within each person, whose natural creativity will be given full expression. The whole human being will be reconstructed, and persons will have earned the right to be called "human beings."

In this chapter we first consider how Marx perceives capitalist economic decline and the ensuing political upheaval and then follow the process by which communism will emerge out of the intervening and temporary state of socialism.

Capitalism under Siege

Capitalism is dynamic. Unless it continues to grow, it will decline. A stationary capitalism is a contradiction in terms. Although the best conditions for the working people are to be found when capitalism is growing, workers suffer whatever its stage. The growth of capital implies the accumulation of larger and larger stocks of capital capable of producing commodities and the further centralization of its control into fewer hands as well. The centralization of capital involves a more minute division of labor and greater use of machinery. The more minute the division of labor, the more the special skills of the laborer become unnecessary. Skilled and semiskilled laborers are replaced with unskilled laborers as tasks are so simplified that anyone can perform them. It is the essence of capitalism that it should employ progressively larger numbers of people with fewer and fewer skills.

The increasing use of capital enabling one worker to produce what until then had been produced by three workers increases competition among workers for jobs that become increasingly scarce. The accumulation of capital also increases competition among capitalists, who are forced to accumulate even more capital. This same accumulation also ruins small manufacturers or producers, who are forced into the ranks of the proletariat.

The rate of interest falls,* reducing the source of income for people of small means and retired people who live on fixed incomes. Ultimately, these people swell the ranks of the proletariat. Finally, in order to survive, capitalists engage in a frenzy of production of goods for sale without respect to any possible market for the ever-increasing supply that the economy is able to produce. This is one cause of a trade crisis.

Every economic crisis hastens an increase in capital accumulation that is self-defeating. The process of accumulation increases competition among workers and capitalists, accelerating the long-run decline in the rate of profit and the reduction in total wage payments to workers.[1] Each surviving capitalist attempts to recover lost profits by further investments in capital (to save labor costs by replacing labor with capital), further depressing the rate of profit. But the incomes of redundant workers are declining even more. In the end, the falling

*The rate of interest can be thought of as a rate of profit.

rate of profit reduces the rate at which further capital can be accumulated, because profits are the source of investment funds.[2]

Falling rates of profit lead to business cycles in the short run and the destruction of capitalism in the long run: "It [a business cycle] promotes overproduction, speculation, crises, surplus-capital [capital capable of producing goods which the poverty-stricken proletariat cannot afford to buy] along with surplus population. Capitalist production becomes a barrier to itself. Production ceases, not because there is no human need for the goods, but because the flawed system of production for profit is no longer capable of continuing."

Political Upheaval and Force

Political upheaval occurs when the productive resources of the existing society are unable to work any longer, bringing the economy to a standstill. However, the productive equipment built under capitalism still stands—ready to be used for the social good. As the power of the ruling class disappears, the "working class will substitute, in the course of development, for the old order of civil society an association which will exclude classes and their antagonism . . . there will no longer be political power, properly speaking, since political power is simply the official form of the antagonism in civil society."

Will there be bloodshed? Under certain conditions. During the period of upheaval, "the antagonism between the proletariat and the bourgeoisie is a struggle between class and class [which] should lead ultimately to a brutal . . . hand-to-hand struggle as its final denouement." Since all political movements are social movements, it is only when class antagonisms disappear that social movements will cease to be political movements. "So in all likelihood there will be a battle to the death between the classes." England might be the exception to the rule: "the only country where the inevitable social revolution might be [achieved] entirely by peaceful and legal means."[3] In general, however, "force is the midwife of every old society pregnant with a new one. [Force] is itself an economic power."[4] If not force, there may be strife. Certainly the use of power is necessary. There is no contradiction, though, in the use of force to bring about social revolution. There is no hard Marxist line on the matter. In Germany, force seemed likely; in France, America, and England, the dying classes might be bought off.

Marx had this to say regarding his conception of the order of change: "What I did that was new was to prove (1) that the existence of classes is only bound up in the particular historical phases in the development of production, (2) that the class struggle necessarily leads to the dictatorship of the proletariat, (3) that the dictatorship itself only constitutes the transition to the abolition of all classes and to a classless society."[5]

Transition

There must be a transition between the death of capitalism and communism. Though Marx sometimes distinguishes between the term "socialism" and "communism" unclearly, socialism can be seen as the link between the death of one and the birth of the other. This is the time period that is marked by the evocative phrase "dictatorship of the proletariat." In Marx's words: "Between capitalist and communist society lies the period of the revolutionary transformation of the one into the other. There corresponds to this also a political transition period in which the state can be nothing but *the revolutionary dictatorship of the proletariat*."[6]

Engels has more to say about this transition in his introduction to *The Civil War in France*, the story of the Paris Commune of 1870. After the Commune was formed in Paris, the entire apparatus of government was reorganized; he notes, "it filled all posts—administrative, judicial, and educational—by election on the basis of universal suffrage of all concerned, subject to the right of recall at any time by the same electors. . . . All officials, high or low, were paid only the wages received by other workers. The highest salary paid by the Commune to anyone was 6000 francs. In this way an effective barrier to place-hunting and careerism was set up, even apart from the binding mandates to delegates to representative bodies which were added besides. . . ."

He goes on to observe that ". . . people think they have taken quite an extraordinarily bold step forward when they have rid themselves of belief in hereditary monarchy and swear by the democratic republic. In reality, however, the state is nothing but a machine for the oppression of one class by another, and indeed in the democratic republic no less than in the monarchy; and at best an evil inherited by the proletariat after its victorious struggle for class supremacy, whose worst sides the victorious proletariat, just like the Commune, cannot avoid having to lop off at once as much as possible until such time as a generation reared in new, free social conditions is able to throw the entire lumber of the state on the scrap heap."[7]

To soften the impact of the idea of dictatorship, Engels writes: "Of late, the Social-Democratic philistine has once more been filled with wholesome terror at the words: Dictatorship of the Proletariat. Well and good, gentlemen, do you want to know what this dictatorship looks like? Look at the Paris Commune. That was the Dictatorship of the Proletariat."[8] Marx and Engels hasten to explain that the dictatorship itself constitutes only the "transition to the *abolition of all classes and to a classless society*."[9]

Engels continues: "Let us see what a socialist economy would look like. Picture a community of free individuals working the means of production together, where the labor power of individuals is consciously organized as labor power for community rather than individuals. All the characteristics of Robinson Crusoe's efforts are reproduced here, except that it is social rather than individual. Everything Crusoe produced was produced by himself alone and for his own use. In our community everything is produced for society. One portion of the output is reinvested and therefore remains social. Another portion is consumed by members of society as their means of subsistence. That portion must be distributed to individuals on some basis. How it is distributed will depend upon where the economy is in terms of its historical development. Let us assume for the sake of this discussion that it is distributed on the basis of labor time. Distribution according to labor time input serves a double purpose. [One purpose is to see to it that producing laborers produce goods in proportion to what the community wants. The other purpose is to be able to measure the worker's input so as to reward the worker with a proper share of the output.] The social relations of the individual producer, with regard both to their labor and to its products, are in this case perfectly simple and intelligible, and that with regard not only to production but also as to distribution."[10]

In the *Critique of the Gotha Programme* Marx chides delegates to a conference in Gotha, Germany, who had met (without Marx) to form the present-day Social Democratic party, for presenting a doctrinally unsound socialist program. Insights into Marx's own ideas about a socialist society are provided by examining his criticism of another approach.

The Gotha program at one point states that *"the proceeds of labor belong undiminished with equal right to all members of society,"* and at another that *"the emancipation of labor demands the promotion of the instruments of labor to the common property of society and the cooperative regulation of the total labor with a fair distribution of the proceeds of labor."*

Marx begins by correcting the language: " 'Promotion of the instruments of labor to the common property' obviously should read their 'conversion into common property.' " He proceeds at his analytical best to shred the remaining parts of that statement and at the same time promote his own views, after remarking that "proceeds of labor" is a loose term subject to a variety of meanings.

Marx asks some rhetorical questions for which he provides the answers. What are the "proceeds of labor"? Are the proceeds the physical output or the value of the output? If it is the value of output that is to be distributed to labor, is all the output to be distributed or only that part newly created by labor? What is meant by a "fair distribution"? Capitalists argue that the distribution of the proceeds of the productive process is "fair" now. Are not economic relationships now determined by legal conceptions? Are not legal conceptions determined in the first place by economic relationships? Is it not true that there are as many interpretations of what is a "fair" distribution as there are socialist sects?

To understand what the term "a fair distribution" really means, Marx argues, one must take the two phrases in the "programme" together. The idea that "the instruments of labor are common property and the total labor is cooperatively regulated" must be combined with the principle that "the proceeds of labor belong undiminished with equal right to all the members of society." Marx asks whether all members of society, working or not, are to share in the output created by those who work. If they are, then the proceeds of labor are not "undiminished." If they aren't, what happens to the rights of *all* members of society?

Aside from that, these are Marx's critical points: It is necessary to deduct from the "full value of the worker's output" the replacement for capital used up in the production process—depreciation. Some output has to be reinvested so as to increase the capital stock of society. Some must be put aside as insurance against unforeseen accidents such as natural calamities.

Marx complains that there is no simple way of determining the size of those deductions. What is left must be further divided between worker consumption (the portion that actually goes to the workers) and that which is necessary for governmental administration and public goods—schools, health services, and so on. The need for public goods grows in proportion as the new society develops. Thus some of the workers' pay comes back to them in the form of public goods.

Finally, before the worker gets the proceeds of his labor, provision must be made for those unable to work. That group includes people on poor relief, the aged, and the disabled. "When all deductions are taken into account, the proceeds of labor that the Gotha Programme has assigned to labor alone has become so diminished that the term has become meaningless."

The Gotha Programme is the program that the Social Democratic party intends to install when it gains power. Marx argues that the proposed program "economically, morally, and intellectually, [is] still stamped with the birthmarks of the old society from whose womb it emerges." The principle that workers get back, after suitable deductions, what they create is the rule for the "exchange of commodities" (the term Marx uses to designate exchange under capitalism).

Under the rule of "equal right" under capitalism, each worker gets what that worker produces, which is "bourgeois right"—not a communist right. Why? Because equal right is in bourgeois society unequal labor. Some people are physically or mentally superior to others and thereby produce more. Labor time, to serve as a measure of output value, must be corrected both for length of working time and the intensity of work. Natural endowments do not justify a greater share of output. Additionally, since some workers are married, with more dependents than others, equal performance (payment according to productive contribution) will mean that some will be richer than others. Marx believes that in order to avoid these defects, rights, instead of being equal, would have to be unequal.

Defects are inevitable in the early stages of communism. "Right" must be conditioned by the stage of cultural and economic development, which is as close as Marx gets to a recommendation concerning the proper distribution of income during the transition. He ends by conceding a qualified acceptance of unequal distribution based on productivity.

Now to Marx's famous dictum about the distribution of income under fully developed communism. "In a higher phase of communist society," he posits, "after the enslaving subordination of the individual in the division of labor, and therewith also the antithesis between mental and physical labor, has vanished; after labor has become not only a means of life but life's prime want; after the productive forces have also increased with the all around development of the individual and all the springs of cooperative wealth flow more abundantly—only then can the narrow horizons of bourgeois right be crossed in its entirety and society inscribe on its banners: From each according to his ability to each according to his needs!"[11]

Communism Triumphant

In the young Marx's *Economic and Philosophic Manuscripts of 1844*, the issue is not yet really economics, but the state of human alienation. Still Hegelian, Marx emphasized the effect of private property relations on the human spirit. Only later did Marx launch into a full-fledged analysis of capitalism, the prime social instrument of human alienation.

Communism abolishes private property. Even in its "crude" form (the transitional socialism discussed earlier) the state may still be democratic or despotic. And even with the disappearance of the state, communism may still be incomplete, still influenced by private property, and alienation may still exist. Also even under conditions of "crude" communism, people do not understand their need to transcend alienation in order to reintegrate their personalities. Because people remain infected with the virus of the private-property ethos, having "grasped its concept, not its essence," they still require the full development of communism to complete their transition back to their true selves.

In a fully developed communist society humans transcend self-estrangement. "Communism therefore is the complete return of man to himself as a social [i.e., human] being." Marx claims further that: "Communism, as fully developed naturalism, equals humanism, and as fully developed humanism equals naturalism; it [is] the genuine resolution of the conflict between man and nature and between man and man—the true resolution of the strife between existence and essence, . . . between freedom and necessity, between the individual and the species. Communism is the riddle of history solved, and it knows itself to be the solution."[12]

When a society based on cooperation is established, and the means of production are owned in common, the labor of the individual as an individual is no longer embodied in products. Laborers work in cooperation with one another so that a product is a joint product. The individual exchange, characteristic of capitalism, no longer occurs.

FREEDOM UNDER COMMUNISM

Freedom does not begin until work is no longer compulsory, that is, compelled from outside. Freedom occurs when people working together determine what they want to produce and how they wish to allocate it, instead of being forced by some "blind" power (presumably the market) to produce and distribute goods as that power wills. Necessary work results will be accomplished "with the least expenditure of energy and under conditions most adequate to [their] human nature and most worthy of it." With necessary goods produced in this manner, people will be able to get beyond economic need and develop the power that is in them to be truly free.[13]

THE DIVISION OF LABOR AND FREEDOM

Marx's description of the possibilities of creative life under communism is perhaps his most visionary statement about the world to come. He always argues that the root of alienation is in the division of labor. The division of labor is necessary in all precommunist societies and is historically not voluntary labor. In all known societies an individual is forced to participate in a "particular, exclusive sphere of activity [from] which he cannot escape. He is a hunter, a fisherman, a shepherd, or a critic, and must remain so if he does not want to lose his means of livelihood."

By contrast, in a communist society, where there is no division of labor, where society regulates what is produced, each person can make whatever contribution he or she wishes to make. It is "possible for me to do one thing today and another tomorrow, to hunt in the morning, fish in the afternoon, rear cattle in the evening, criticize after dinner, just as I have a mind without becoming hunter, fisherman, shepherd, or critic."[14]

How the Proletarian Revolution Solves
Capitalist Contradictions

When the proletariat seizes power, it socializes the means of production. Once this occurs, the benefits of socialism can work freely because it is possible to plan production and distribution. Classes are rendered obsolete. As the anarchy of production vanishes, the political authority of the state wanes. Humans gain control over their own society and at the same time become lords of Nature. People become their own masters, free at last. The historical mission of the proletariat is to achieve universal emancipation. The task of the communist movement as a whole, workers and intellectuals, is to see historical processes clearly and to see the historical necessity of the proletarian revolution.[15]

The Economy under Communism

Prices

Marx supports the proposition that in the long run the prices of products should equal their "natural" prices. In this position, Marx follows David Ricardo. In the short run, according to Ricardo, a price may be above or below its "natural" level, that is, above or below its costs of production. This situation occurs because social demand may at any moment be greater or less than its supply. Rational policy makers will adjust supply or demand, so that its market price in the long run will be equal to its "natural" price. Ricardo—and Marx, his student in economics—assumed that the costs of production included wages and profits. But unlike Ricardo, Marx sees profits as a capitalist device to annex some of the income received from the sale of a commodity wholly created by labor power for the benefit of the capitalist. Profits therefore really "belong" to laborers who created the product, not to capitalists. However, Marx's theory of value (that is, his theory of how prices are formed) is the same as Ricardo's and he expects that theory to operate after the revolution. "The exchange, or sale, of commodities at their value," he writes, "is the rational way, the natural law of their equilibrium."[16]

Money

Under "socialized production" money is to disappear. Society allocates labor power and the means of production, according to plan, to the production of different goods. In place of money, people will receive paper checks equal in value to their labor-time input. This will enable the worker to "withdraw from the social supply" goods for consumption. Marx does not see these paper checks as money because they do not circulate.[17]

PLANNING

When society is master of all of its means of production and uses them according to a social plan, it eliminates forever the subjugation of people to their own means of production. Society is not free unless every person in that society is free. Therefore the old modes of production must be revolutionized from top to bottom. And of course, the old division of labor must disappear. Production must be organized so that no one person can shift the burden of production to the shoulders of another.

The sharing of the burden of work is the natural condition of human existence. It is the way in which productive labor, instead of enslaving individuals, becomes the means of their emancipation. It is the means whereby "each person is thereby enabled to develop all his facilities, physical and mental, in all directions and exercise them to the full—in which [situation] therefore, productive labor will become a pleasure instead of a burden."[18]

When society seizes the means of production, capitalist production disappears, and with it mastery by the capitalist producer. The anarchy of production, responsible for business crises, is replaced by systematic organization. The struggle for existence on the part of individuals disappears. Then, for the first time, mankind is clearly differentiated from the animal and emerges into a really human existence.

The whole environment that has up to now ruled human life then comes under human dominion. People become the masters of nature because they master their own social organization. The laws of social action—taken falsely to be laws of nature—will now be fully understood, mastered, and put to human uses.

Social organizations previously accepted as historical necessities of nature are now created by means of the free actions of people themselves. Forces that have until now governed history now come under human control. As time goes on, "man himself, more and more consciously, [will] make his own history. . . ." The social causes set in motion by humans will result in outcomes desired by them. "It [fully developed communism] is the ascent of man from the kingdom of necessity to the kingdom of freedom."[19]

Only when society is able to make its productive forces dovetail harmoniously into one another according to a single vast plan will it be possible to distribute industry over the entire country "in the way best adapted to its own development, and to the maintenance and development of the other elements of production."[20]

The State under Communism

When the power of the forces of production is understood and brought under control, Marx believes it can be cooperatively transformed by producers working together. The difference between an economy under capitalism and communism is comparable to the difference between the destructive force of electricity in the lightning of the storm and electricity under control in telegraphy and the voltaic arc; "the difference between a conflagration, and fire working in the service of man."

When the working people understand the power of productive forces, the social anarchy in the production of income and wealth gives way to the regulation of production by a definite plan, according to the needs of the community and each individual. The capitalist mode of production, which enslaves first the producer and then the capitalist who appropriates the product, is replaced by a form of appropriation of the output based on the modern means of production. Consequently society will appropriate some of the output for the maintenance and increase of the capital stock and some for the direct use of individuals for subsistence and enjoyment.

Whereas the capitalist mode of production progressively transforms the masses into proletarians, it creates the power that causes capitalism to destroy itself, thereby making revolution inevitable. It is at this point, according to Marx, that the proletariat seizes political power and turns the means of production into state property.

In so doing it abolishes itself as a proletariat, abolishes all class distinctions, and abolishes the state as a state. Societies based on class antagonisms have historically needed a state, that is, an organization of the ruling class that was temporarily exploiting the proletariat. The purpose of that organization was to prevent any external interference with the existing conditions of production. Its further purpose was to keep the exploited classes permanently oppressed. While the state appeared to be the official representative of society as a whole, its visible embodiment, it was really the representative of the class that it served. In ancient times it was the state of slave-owning citizens; in the Middle Ages, the feudal lords; in our own time, the bourgeoisie. When finally it becomes the real representative of the whole society, it renders itself unnecessary.

As soon as there is no social class to be held in subjection; as soon as class rule and the struggle for existence necessitating the present anarchy of production and the conflict consequent to it is removed, "nothing remains to be repressed, and a special repressive force, a state, is no longer necessary."

The first act of the state, after the revolution, is to constitute itself a representative of the whole society, and to take possession of the means of production in the name of society. The first act "is also its last independent act as a state. State interference in social relations becomes superfluous in one domain after another. . . . the government of persons is replaced by the administration of things, and by the conduct of processes of production. The state is not 'abolished.' *It dies out.*"[21]

Summary

We have shown in earlier chapters that capitalism comes to an end because of its inner contradictions. Specifically, capitalism ends because the source of surplus value, the profit of capitalists (which is living labor), is continually replaced by constant capital (machinery and equipment). On the one hand, the productive capacity of the economy is fully developed; on the other, it is unable to provide profits for capitalists because living labor has been replaced by constant capital. In addition, since most workers are in the reserve army of the unemployed, they have no source of income with which to buy produced commodities. For both reasons, the engine of capitalism breaks down. On the social side, the misery of the working class has increased beyond endurance—both because they are poorer than ever relative to the capitalists and because they are alienated from themselves, from one another, and—of course—from capitalists.

The scene is set for political upheaval, which may take the form of revolution or may take the form of a peaceful political reversal. In either case the communist revolution should succeed rather easily because the capitalists have been demoralized and their system has broken down. With the revolution, classes come to an end. They are succeeded by a dictatorship of the proletariat. This dictatorship of the proletariat is a transitional phase between capitalism and a classless society.

Under communism, people are free. They are free from the necessity to work for subsistence, to compete, to struggle against nature, to struggle against one another, to struggle against oppressors. The division of labor disappears; each person produces products for use and not for sale, though they exchange surplus products with others. People are no longer specialists, but many-sided generalists. One no longer lives to work; rather, one lives to develop one's personality and capacities to their fullest. People can realize their true natures, which are many-sided and encompass a wide range of interests and activities.

In communist society, money disappears; goods are exchanged according to the value of the labor that is contained in them. The economy is organized "rationally"; business cycles disappear, and control over the economy rests in human hands. Human beings, who have up to this time been controlled by natural and extraneous historical forces, now themselves control human and nonhuman forces. History presumably comes to an end. The goals to which all history has been pointing are achieved.

We have completed an exegesis of the Marxist System from its beginning in Hegel's idealism and in the rational thought of the Enlightenment to its promise of a better tomorrow for all. The Marxist System comprised a theory of history, of motivation, of social analysis, of economic analysis, and a vision of the future—an astonishing intellectual achievement. Still Marx's insight into the way the social world operates, internally consistent as it is, has its shortcomings, as our brief Evaluation, Summary, and Critique in chapter 12 indicates. And of course the continued triumph of capitalism in the West and the decline of Marxist prestige in the East do not suggest that Marx's objective, to create a civilization "worthy of man," is on the immediate horizon.

Marx was a friend of humankind and wished it well. Like all intellectuals influenced by Enlightenment thought, he believed that human nature was essentially good, that the individual was capable of self-development as a loving, cooperative, and kindly member of society. Only a hostile world environment prevented such self-realization. Above all, he believed that each human being would someday be free to develop his or her creative self almost limitlessly.

Like other post-Enlightenment figures, Marx did not view humans as "reasoning" animals and thereby perfectible through the development of their capacity to reason. Marx rejected as "utopian" such views, which were held by the French philosophers, Robert Owen, and others. Rather, Marx saw people as creatures of an environment that they were ultimately capable of transcending, but by which the human personality was fundamentally molded in spirit and deed. A person's ability to reason was conditioned by circumstances.

Marx, building on his earlier Hegelian leanings, believed that history had a direction and a purpose. Although critical of Hegel for arguing that history developed toward perfection in the human mind, Marx accepted Hegel's basic conception of the inevitability of progress toward a perfect world through the unfolding of history in the real world. History was made in the real, or "material," world, not in the mind's world of ideas. History was made by men, "but not just as they pleased."

That the goal of freedom would be achieved, in the fullness of time with the achievement of communism, was an article of faith with Marx. The communist world was specifically a world without social classes and therefore without coercive power; a world of abundance and therefore without strife and competitiveness; a world without the necessity to make choices (among scarce goods, perhaps, but probably not in social life, although Marx is not explicit). *Spontaneity* and *full self-development* would be hallmarks of the world to come.

The modern observer has doubts about most of this vision. Although agreeing that history is made by real people, in real circumstances not wholly under their control, most thinking contemporaries would disagree with the no-tion that history has a "purpose." Or if there is a purpose, it is not one we can know. Contemporary evidence hardly supports the concept of the inevitability of human progress. We live in a deeply pessimistic time.

The next chapter deals with a critique of a few of the significant positions taken by Marx. It is by no means a comprehensive criticism of Marx. That task has been undertaken by others.

CHAPTER 12

EVALUATION, SUMMARY, AND CRITIQUE

Marxism as an ideology and a method of analysis is based on the German historical and romantic tradition. Its evolutionary optimism follows the tradition of Hegel and his intellectual predecessors, the Enlightenment thinkers in Germany and Western Europe. The central event that engaged Marx's imagination was the industrial revolution (and its political counterpart, the French Revolution). That event ignited a demand for bourgeois democracy and capitalism. The concern that motivated Marx's passionate and brilliant analysis was the gross inequality of power, money, and status that accompanied the economics and politics of the shift from an agricultural to a manufacturing society in Europe.

Marx assumed that all the ingredients of a full-fledged industrial system were in place in Britain and France—advanced technology, money capital, a free labor force, and a natural environment (land) released from feudal restrictions. He also believed the "superstructure" in both countries was fully developed. In his larger vision Marx saw the superstructure as including scientific knowledge, specifically that of the newly emerging natural, biological, and social sciences. By blending his comprehensive understanding of knowledge as it existed during the middle years of the nineteenth century with his overarching vision of the human condition, he developed the Marxist System. Armed with its tenets, Marx then analyzed past human history and boldly predicted the future.

The faults of Marxism are in part those that are the fate of all sweeping theoretical structures. They promise more than they can deliver, particularly when they claim more than scientific evidence warrants.

Marx stimulated the thought of countless thousands of other investigators, who, whether critics or supporters, were energized by the audacity of his inquiry and the promise of his method. Great scientists stimulate the thought of others and inspire them to activity.

No scientist ever really expects a newly discovered theory either to explain a phenomenon "fully" or to stand unchallenged. The claim that one theory is superior to another is no more than a claim that the superior theory has greater explanatory value than its alternative.

For modern critics, the Marxist System is an easy intellectual target. Marx's sweeping claim to a holistic theory of social behavior is pretentious. His vast and premature conclusions were based on social and scientific theories still in their infancy. He remained an optimist long after the Enlightenment faith in the possibilities open to humanity was in decline. Worse, his image of what a utopia should be like is flawed in ways to be discussed in this chapter.

In this chapter, I deal with some of the major grounds for criticism of the Marxist System, beginning with a discussion of Marx's utopia. Following that discussion, I evaluate several other of his major ideas, concluding with some speculation on the future of Marxism under late-twentieth-century conditions.

The Marxist Utopia

Marx's concept of utopia envisions human freedom as a condition in which individuals, released from need, develop their creative potential to the utmost. Of central importance, there is no longer a division of labor. Without a division of labor, there are neither specialists nor alienated workers. The well-organized (planned) industrial machine, liberated from its capitalist overlords, runs with minimal voluntary supervision. With the problem of production thus solved, distribution requires only moderate restraint by consumers. There is plenty for all. In social affairs without conflict, there is little need of government. Crime is abolished and war is obsolete, for there is nothing to be gained by theft or conquest.

Marx's image of freedom assumes, as already noted, a world in which there is no need to make choices in economic or political affairs. But even were an economy of abundance achievable, this concept of freedom is subject to extensive criticism.[1]

To begin with, it can be argued that spontaneous self-development is not enough for a meaningful life, that people need goals outside themselves. Since in communism nothing of value is scarce, persons need not strive for anything. No difficult choices must be made. But as John Schaar says, "To live is to choose." Freedom involves discipline, "reasoned rejection of some alternatives in favor of others." Without external goals, he continues, "life becomes its own end and product, the goal and good in itself" and "is aimless, adrift in its own existence . . . is empty [filled with] frivolities and busyness . . . as if these could fill the void left by lack of purpose."[2]

Furthermore, even if the economic problem of a relative scarcity of goods in relation to wants was solved, other and more fundamental values might not be realized. A satiated demand for goods and freedom from "forced" labor do not guarantee an absence of desire for other scarce values including power, prestige, acceptance, and possibly domination. Neither all good nor all evil is economically motivated. Unless one accepts the doubtful thesis that people are inherently selfless and without ambition, there must be conflicts of interests and goals other than economic.

The truth is, of course, that power, status, and money will never be available to all in limitless amounts. And there are few who foresee an end to the necessity for human striving. For better or worse, most people would concede that to be human is to have to make choices in pursuit of scarce values.

Alienation

The concept of alienation, the touchstone of Marx's social criticism, is closely associated with his definition of freedom. For Marx, whose primary concern is the consequences of economic and social arrangements for the human spirit, to be alienated is to lack freedom.

The young Marx of the *Economic and Philosophic Manuscripts of 1844* argues that the source of alienation is the division of labor. Alienation occurs because of the *need* to produce for a living, which Marx called "forced labor." In that formulation freedom and unalienated labor are the same. And in communism both are achieved simultaneously.

The view of alienation most often associated with Marxism has less to do with the *process* of production and the division of labor than with the question of distribution. Who receives the gains from commodity exchange? The Marxist critique of capitalism rests on the appropriation by capitalists of the output of laborers, the unfair division of produced output. So perceived, alienation is the same as exploitation.

If the division of labor, clearly necessary for efficient production, is the main cause of alienation, can or should alienation ever be overcome? The problem with connecting alienation to exploitation is that it regards payments for the use of nonhuman inputs such as land and capital as illegitimate. Mainstream economists believe that resources cannot be used most effectively if the prices of these resources do not reflect their scarcity in relation to the claims on their services. We address that question below.

CLASSES

The division of labor also results in the formation of classes. To eliminate classes would be to resolve the twin problems of alienation and exploitation. But a rather plausible argument can be made that just as it is utopian to expect an eventual end to alienation, so it is unrealistic to expect the end of classes, at least in the sense of differential power and responsibility, creativity, and reward.

It is not necessarily true that differentials in power and status, if functional, inevitably lead to struggles among classes. An older view of class, one held by Aristotle, for example, is that classes complement one another, providing a mutually satisfying division of labor and responsibility. And if the resulting differentials in power are functional, they will survive the demise of private property. Power relationships necessarily develop in complex societies where all social activity requires delegation of responsibilities for decision making and supervision. Property ownership is not the only source of differences in power and income. Power derives from institutional position. Leaders in business, politics, education, military service, and so on, derive power from leadership in large organizations, which can arise from rare expertise, personal effectiveness, or a generally good reputation for wisdom or virtue.

Marx's emphasis on classes has sparked endless debate and research. For one thing, he never defined the "boundaries." Who belongs to which class? Are classes identified by occupation, by wealth, by status? Marx locates class according to position in the economy. He puts economic status first. Max Weber (1864-1920), arguably Germany's greatest modern sociologist, locates classes according to power. There appear to be multiple sources of power.

Some contemporary social scientists emphasize a plurality of interests and power relationships and claim, as a result, that there is no single dominant class. Others argue that competition among elites within the same class eliminates interclass conflict. And there are those who trivialize the concept of class, defining class as a matter of social behavior and life styles. Then there are those who accept the existence of classes but see no evidence that they are, as Marx predicted, becoming more and more "polarized."

Perhaps the problem is that persons do not identify themselves with a particular class. The working class has never become a class "for itself," a group of people who identify themselves as working class with a common agenda. This has been especially true in the United States and some other highly industrialized countries. Marx thought of classes objectively, materialistically; that is, classes exist and persons are class members whether they realize that fact or not. To simplify social analysis for maximum political effect, when he and Engels wrote the *Manifesto,* Marx chose a two-class model. The conflict of the two main classes, the bourgeoisie and proletariat, would change history.

Marx by his own proclamation wrote philosophy to help change the world, not simply to explain it. He himself never analyzed the questions raised by his use of class analysis. It is important to realize that the real struggle that he and Engels described in the *Manifesto* was between two powerful classes, a declining landed aristocracy and an emerging bourgeoisie, not bourgeoisie and proletariat.

An important question, still debated, is the relationship between classes in a political democracy. Marx's concept of freedom meant, ultimately, the elimination of power relationships. The classless society that Marx envisioned would be a mass society of equals. A classless society is a democratic form closer to the tradition of Rousseau, the philosopher of the French Revolution, than to the tradition of John Locke, the philosopher of the Glorious Revolution of 1688 in England. Locke saw a mass society of equals as a danger to everyone's freedom. He placed his trust in rule by the better classes, squires and landed aristocrats, rather than by merchants and manufacturers. Rule by ordinary people was unthinkable. From Locke is derived the principle of equality of opportunity. The American political system of representative government accepts the Lockean tradition; the political systems of Eastern Europe are influenced by Marx, the Rousseauean.

The philosophy of Jean Jacques Rousseau (1712–78) emphasized equality of social condition of all citizens (rather than simply equality of opportunity), whose collective or general will, the dynamic of the nation, would be embodied in a leader.

Exploitation

The definition of exploitation by mainstream economists, derived from neoclassical economics, is payment to workers below the value of their "marginal product." Crudely, it is paying workers less than their contribution to the sale price (or value added at the margin) of the product.

It is Marx's view that the source of all profit, rent, and interest payments is exploited labor, which is the only source of surplus value. The assertion that living labor is the source of all value is an a priori assumption, of course, not a scientifically proven truth. And Marx's central position, that profit rates will fall as capital replaces labor in the productive process, depends heavily on that assumption.

If, as mainstream economists believe, nonhuman factors of production such as land and capital contribute to the production of output and therefore "earn" a portion of the income arising from the sale of commodities, some of the moral sting of Marx's observation that capitalists appropriate what has been produced by labor alone is lost. Followers of Marx are certain that the assignment of credit to nonhuman factors of production by late-nineteenth-century economists was motivated by fear of the implications of Marxism for the legitimacy of private property and enterprise. And they rightly argue that there is no proof that "factors" of production are indeed paid the value of their contribution to the value of output at the margin (the value of their marginal product).

Questioning the validity of the labor theory of value is a challenge to the Marxist position that widely unequal income distribution is arbitrary and due to unbalanced political power. On the other hand, it is not clear that owners of nonhuman factors of production have a moral right to the vast incomes accruing to them. The mainstream argument for inequality of income is functional, although often justified on moral grounds. Efficient production and economic growth are said to require inequality of income, and people have a "right" to what they earn. Even if Marx's theory of value was wrong, present justifications for vast social inequality are on grounds that are shaky from the point of view of both morality and economic efficiency.

Marxist Science

Science is best understood as a method of trying to learn something undeniable about the real world. An acceptable scientific theory must pass two tests. It must, at least in principle, be subject to verifiability. That is, it must be possible to devise a test, even an abstract test if an experiment is not possible, that could disprove the theory. And it must be able to predict events more accurately and more widely than an alternative theory.

Marx believed that his work was scientific because the dialectical method and the labor theory of value provided useful assumptions from which he could reason. He thought that his assumption that history worked dialectically permitted him to deduce the reality of socioeconomic processes that lay behind their deceptive appearances. Dialectical materialism helped Marx understand things about the world that he thought were undeniable, and the labor theory of value enabled him to predict the eventual end of capitalism.

The problem with Marxism as science is not that both assumptions are erroneous. An assumption need not be proved. But, in general, a better assumption provides a base from which to reason to conclusions of greater predictive value. The problem with Marx's science is that its most important postulate, the inevitable decline of capitalism, cannot be disproved by test. The longevity of capitalism does not disprove the theory. Marx did take the precaution of speaking of "counteracting tendencies." When can it be said that those tendencies that delay a decline in the rate of profit no longer obtain? Capitalism may inevitably decline, but Marx's theory cannot be faulted whether or not capitalism ever disappears. All that we know from the evidence of what has occurred is that the fortunes of capitalism ebb and flow.

Marxism's standing as science cannot be impaired by denying the two major assumptions from which it is derived. The most important way that a theory dies is from neglect. That can occur when another theory reasons to different or more general conclusions from another set of assumptions. Ultimately the "better" theory prevails.

Contemporary mainstream economists theorize that the rate of profit need not decline. Neoclassical economic theory, born as early as the 1870s, convinced most economists that capitalism will not necessarily decline. Marxist economists, a small minority of present-day professional economists, remain convinced that Marx's economic theory better explains economic phenomena than do current versions of neoclassical theory. Marxist economists expect the rate of profit to decline and socialism to emerge triumphant.

The dialectical method of analysis appeals to the modern mind because it places dynamic change, rather than stasis, as the central element of history. Life is an ongoing process; the world is always in the process of becoming, never in equilibrium, never at rest. The dialectical process, for Marx, explained how the world changed. He saw life as a process energized by conflict. Adam Smith, whom supporters of capitalism naturally prefer, saw life as proceeding according to the principle of cooperation and harmony because of the common interests shared by labor and capital. Again, the issue is not whether the assumption of dialectical materialism is correct, but whether that assumption makes it possible to explain more or less of human history. As a single assumption, dialectical materialism bears a large burden.

Marx's method is scientific and his conclusions and interpretation of events are more plausible than those of many others during and since his time. Far into the nineteenth century, for instance, economists were still convinced that overpopulation in the West threatened its stability when all evidence was to the contrary.

Marx can be criticized for mixing science and politics. The whole point of theory is to inform practice. Marx the scientist was more cautious than Marx the political leader. In the latter capacity especially, he was likely to attract followers, particularly the Russian revolutionaries, who rushed impatiently to change the world—with dire consequences.

Using a highly simplified theory based on questionable assumptions as a guide to action carries dangers not dissimilar to those facing a motorist who follows a road map as though there were no traffic or traffic lights, potholes, buildings, and slippery pavement. Yet theories that are simple and abstract have greater explanatory value for more phenomena than those that are complex and detailed.

MORALITY

Marx's theory of history has had practical political consequences, as he had hoped it would. For him, history comes to an end only when humans are perfect beings. Forcing a society to organize to be perfect, by whatever means at hand, is moral if, according to some Marxists, the goal is the creation of perfect people.

Implied in Marx's theory of history is the mischievous doctrine that knowledge of what is moral can, like other knowledge about the universe, be derived scientifically. By accepting the view that morality can be deduced from what seems to be necessary in history, Leninists and Stalinists justified sacrificing entire populations toward ends that they said history required.

But from unprovable, even wrong, assumptions, good theories of society and proper behavior can sometimes result. The freedoms built into the U.S. Constitution are derived from natural law. The Declaration of Independence declares that it is "self-evident" that "all men are created free and equal," and that society should be organized to assure the reality of that truth, otherwise government would be in violation of the wishes of the "author of the universe." Neither the historical purposes of the universe, according to Hegel and Marx, nor the necessities of nature in natural-law theories (attributed to Aristotle and his followers) are scientifically supportable.

Good consequences have also resulted from Marxist moral criticism. Marx brought into sharp focus the kind of false and self-serving morality that springs from self-interest, that serves to comfort the privileged while confusing and silencing the victims of injustice.

Marx's purpose was to promote a true morality based on equality and justice. Nevertheless, to declare morality to be part of the material universe (or to be the will of God) is to lend authority to a particular set of values whose morality should, like all other questions of value, be a matter of debate.

Capitalism: Value and Price

Marxism provides two strands of analysis, one moral and the other economic, both of which are meant to serve humane purposes. Marx wishes to show that the exploitative relationship between bourgeoisie and proletariat, owner and worker, is both spiritual and material.

The labor theory of value combines them both. For that reason, the *assumption* of the labor theory of value is central to the Marxist System. The moral content of that assumption challenges the legitimacy of any system of private property. Once the labor theory of value is abandoned, as it has been by most "bourgeois" economists, an important criticism of the inequities of the capitalist system is blunted.

The assumption of a labor theory of value creates difficulties for the scientist wishing to validate Marx's theories of how capitalism operates. How can an investigator discover whether the rate of profit is declining because the content of living labor used in production is falling relative to constant capital if all that can be observed are the prices of inputs that may be above or below "value"? Values that may be above or below prices are unobservable. Profit rates may be falling or rising without any observable relationship to labor (or *necessary* labor) or capital content. An investigator cannot show that the vital equation expressing a rate of profit, $S/(C + V)$, is diminishing or increasing for the reasons that Marx posits. The labor theory of value is not testable.

A theory must always confront several questions: In the end, does it have more explanatory value than its competitors? Can it predict an event better than its alternatives? Is it simpler, and does it have wider application than others? Does, for instance, the labor theory of value tell us more about the way the economy operates than neoclassical economics does? At present, the bulk of opinion among economists is that the shortcomings of the labor theory of value outweigh its advantages. Subjective theories of value (those based on demand rather than supply) have been in the intellectual ascendancy for more than a century. But in economics, as in all science, there is always more to be said.

Capitalism: Crises and Breakdown

Crises get worse over time because fewer and fewer workers are needed to operate ever more productive capital equipment and therefore living labor, the source of surplus value, dries up. The assumption of a labor theory of value requires this result. There should be evidence of long-run increases in unemployment (the development of a reserve army). For this there is currently no evidence. If capitalism is ultimately to decline, there should also be evidence of ever-deepening recessions followed by weaker recoveries. This also has not been observed.

Marx's understanding of the causes of crises was probably an advance over the explanations of the classical economists of his time. Business-cycle theory owes much to Marx. He identified the existence of trade cycles and offered new analyses of them. Theories of the business cycle, during the latter part of the nineteenth century and the first three decades of the twentieth century, were not helpful in controlling the cycles. It is only in relatively recent years that John Maynard Keynes and his supporters and critics, by investigation and theoretical argument, have made some, if not overwhelming, progress toward an understanding of the causes and remedies for business cycles. In the West since World War II, the amplitude of cycles has been moderated from the earlier part of the century. But theoretical attempts to explain business cycles remain unconvincing.

Unlike some interpretations of the theories of Keynes in the 1940s and 1950s, which postulated that the economy had a tendency to underemployment equilibrium, rehabilitated neoclassical economic theory has revived the concept that the long-term "tendency" in the economy is toward full employment and nonaccelerating prices. Just as Marx's "counteracting tendencies" to the theory that the rate of profit will ultimately decline is not useful in predicting the decline of capitalism, the recently revived and refurbished neoclassical doctrine that capitalist economies have "tendencies" to full employment in the long run is not useful for societies suffering stagnation and unemployment. A "tendency" without a date remains a sterile, unusable theory.

Marxism is old-fashioned in that modern economic theory has surpassed Marx's work in technical virtuosity. But many people do not have a high degree of confidence in the capability of modern macroeconomic theory to help policy makers provide more than simple controls over the economy, let alone explain or predict prices or the level of economic activity and employment.

The Future of Socialism

Marx has continuing appeal for some Western intellectuals who dislike capitalist civilization with its inequities and insecurities and who distrust those relatively few private persons into whose hands so much power and wealth have fallen. But there are few who celebrate the achievements of so-called Marxist societies, which have been painfully meager. After more than 200 years of protest directed against the human costs of the industrial revolution, to this day there exists no useful theory of socialist economic and social organization.

Some Eastern European economies have prospered in recent years to the extent that they have moved away from a rigid, centrally controlled organization of the economy. Wherever the market has been reintroduced in Eastern Europe or China, the economy has burst with new life. And certainly it is not clear that Marx himself would have organized an economy with the high degree of rigidity found in the USSR and through imitation (and fear) found in nearby people's republics. But Marx's hostility to markets and the "anarchy" of production that he saw consequent to their existence established Marx as a bitter critic of market capitalism and a prophet of centrally planned economies. Further, in view of his belief that the source of alienation was found in the division of labor, the sine qua non of a market economy, he could hardly have supported a market presence as an adjunct to any successor system to capitalism.

It is interesting that all that seems to remain of the Marxist vision in people's republics is rhetorical reference to Marxism. Whether any people in leadership positions still believe in the imminent collapse of capitalism or the creation of a society "worthy of man" seems doubtful.

Lenin's attempt to convert Marxism, which was originally designed for developed societies in search of justice and equality, into a system designed to speed economic growth in Third World countries has been a disastrous failure. Few, probably, are the remaining apologists for Lenin's vision. The people of Eastern Europe have shown that when given a chance, they would smite their oppressors hip and thigh.

The socialist vision, hardly an invention of Marx's, appears to be unreachable by means of social systems that Marxism has inspired. Capitalism is, of course, hardly an ideal alternative. Capitalism, on its record in the West and the Pacific rim, creates wealth and offers freedom for individuals. But it offers economic efficiency, not equality. Marx was right to believe that under capitalism people with money get more justice, education, and medical attention and live longer than those without. The system does not distribute its fruits very well and its inequities seem intractable. The trick that Marxists have not been able to pull off would have been to hitch the capitalist engine of economic growth to the socialist wagon of equality and justice.

Marxism's day appears to be over. As a political program that can appeal even to countries of the Third World, its dismal record of failure with regard to the elimination of poverty and the guarantee of human rights will doubtless hasten its demise. Marxism will continue to appeal to some intellectuals because there is no other systematic critical theory of capitalism. Criticism abhors, so it seems, a theoretical lacuna.

Marxism will settle into its important historical niche. Like the Roman Empire, it will be gone if not forgotten, but its consequences will endure. Its failure to unify theory and practice means that Hercules will finally put Antaeus to rest.

Following my consideration of the Marxist System as it has evolved since Marx's day, it seems appropriate to take a look at the life of Marx, perhaps the most influential intellectual in modern history. Certainly he would challenge Charles Darwin for primacy as "The Man of the Nineteenth Century." But his life itself, as the reader can see in the next two chapters, was conventional and quite without the heroic dimensions that might be expected of a person whose writings would influence the world for generations to come.

CHAPTER 13

MARX AS A YOUNG MAN

Karl Marx was born on 5 May 1818 in Trier, at that time part of Prussia, now in West Germany.[1] Marx's grandfather, Marx Levi, who was a rabbi in Trier, dropped the Levi from the family name. He and his wife, Eva, had many children, and Hirschel, Marx's father, was born in 1782. A highly regarded lawyer, in 1824 he became a Christian and took the name of Heinrich Marx. He died in 1838. His wife, Henrietta, who lived until 1863, came from a long line of rabbis. In their large family, Karl was the eldest male, and his childhood was carefree and reasonably affluent.

Heinrich Marx, a child of the Enlightenment, was liberal in politics, although he was a Prussian patriot, supporting the unification of Germany under the leadership of the Prussian Frederick William III. After the spread of liberal ideas brought about by the Napoleonic conquest, it became possible for Jews to join the mainstream of intellectual life and enter most professional occupations. In Trier, in the atmosphere of eighteenth-century rationalism, Marx's father was one of a fair number of Jews who took advantage of the opportunities to convert to Christianity. They acted in response to the anti-Semitism of the day, which required a Jew to become a Christian to be socially accepted.

Among Heinrich Marx's Christian neighbors was Ludwig von Westphalen, whose forebears had distinguished themselves in a variety of political struggles. Westphalen, an intelligent, warm, and open man, befriended Karl as a young boy, and their discussions during long walks were important in Karl's intellectual growth. Karl Marx always spoke of Ludwig von Westphalen with reverence and gratitude.

Karl fell in love with Ludwig's daughter, Jenny, who was born 12 February 1814, and though the Westphalen family considerably outranked the Marx family, and though the Marxes were still thought of as Jews, Ludwig acceded to the marriage, which took place in 1843 when Marx was twenty-five years old. By all accounts, the marriage was a happy one. Jenny became a dedicated revo-

137

lutionary who followed her husband intellectually as well as geographically all through their long and strenuous lives. When she died, two years before Marx, in 1881, it is said that her husband's interest in life disappeared along with her.

The couple had six children, three of whom died young, during the period of abysmal poverty that the Marx family endured as exiles in London. Three of his daughters grew to maturity, two marrying French revolutionaries, the third marrying an English socialist. Because most of Marx's adult life was spent as an exile in England, his children thought of themselves as English. In addition to the immediate family, the Marxes had a housekeeper, Helene Demuth, who lived with them throughout their life together and with whom Marx had an illegitimate child, a scandal that was kept very quiet during his lifetime. Upon the death of both of the older Marxes, Helene went to live with Frederick Engels.

The inner circle of the Marx family included Frederick Engels, whom Marx first met in Paris and with whom he collaborated from 1845 until his death. Engels was more than a collaborator; he supported the Marxes all their lives. The son of a wealthy German manufacturer, he worked for the family firm of Erman and Engels in Manchester until 1870. He then sold out his interest in the business and received enough money to support himself and Marx in modest circumstances. Without Engels's support as a friend and confidant Marx could not have survived, and of all his contemporaries and collaborators, Engels was the only one in whom he placed full trust and confidence.

Student Days

After graduating from high school in Trier, in 1835, Karl studied law at Bonn University and became engaged to Jenny von Westphalen. After one year at Bonn, he transferred to Berlin University to continue the study of jurisprudence at the request of his father, who was concerned about establishing a career for his extraordinary son. Instead of attending classes, however, Marx read voluminously in history and philosophy, falling under the influence of Georg Wilhelm Friedrich Hegel, the reigning philosopher of his day. Marx joined the Young Hegelians, who saw the revolutionary potential in the Hegelian doctrine of the dialectical process by which history continues to evolve toward the Absolute. The Young Hegelians were attracted by Hegelian methods, rather than by Hegel's philosophy, and saw the process of dialectical change as revolutionary in that the old forms were destroyed through the contradictions spawned within them. The new synthesis was always an improvement in the human condition. These revolutionary implications of the doctrine were not lost on Marx.

Typically, Marx did not bother with the formalities of receiving his degree from Berlin University, but given the necessity of earning a living, gained a degree in absentia from yet another school, Jena University. He had anticipated an academic career in Germany. But because of the radicalism of his sponsor, Bruno Bauer, who had also been associated with the Young Hegelians, and changes in the political situation in Prussia, an academic career was closed to Marx.

Marx the Journalist

In 1841, after failing to receive an academic appointment, Marx became a contributor to and then editor of the *Deutsche Jahrbücher*, together with Arnold Ruge. In 1842, he moved to Cologne to contribute to and later edit the *Rheinische Zeitung*. Marx was not at this time a communist, and when a competitive paper accused him of not understanding communism, he admitted his ignorance and promised to study communist theory in depth and to report his findings in the *Rheinische Zeitung*. Meanwhile, the newspaper was continually censored by the government because of its criticism of existing orthodoxies with respect to press freedom, the theft of wood by the poor, religion, marriage, divorce laws, philosophy, poverty, revolution, and the reactionary practices of both the Prussian monarchy of William IV and the Russian czar.

Marx responded to government pressure to moderate his views by ignoring it, with the result that the government completely suppressed the newspaper. Marx then left Prussia, never to resume permanent residence there, maintaining that "there's nothing more I can do in Germany. One debases oneself here." As it happened, Marx was never allowed to return permanently to Germany and was ultimately forced to renounce his citizenship.

In Paris, Ruge had organized a second periodical, the *Deutsche-Französische Jahrbücher*, which was to realize the "Gallo-Germanic Principle." Its sole double-volume publication appeared in February 1844. Although Ruge, Mikhail Bakunin, and Ludwig Feuerbach also made contributions, the most notable contribution to its pages was by Marx, who made a sharp break with the idealism of Hegel and established the foundations of historical materialism. Under the influence of Feuerbach, Marx linked his belief in social change and dynamic progress to change in the material conditions under which human beings lived. In his article on the "Jewish Question," which was a response to Bruno Bauer, he gave preliminary form to a materialist conception of history. Bauer had argued that Jews cannot become citizens in a Gentile world until they give up their Jewishness and become Gentiles. Only in that way can they become free. In contrast, Marx argued that Jews can become free only with the emancipation of all mankind. Bauer saw the Jewish Question as religious, Jews being "free" Christians in a state of arrested development. For Bauer, only the state could emancipate Jews, and the state was Christian. For Marx, the state was a manifestation of the bourgeois society that created it, and emancipation would come only when state and society were severed. Unlike Hegel, on whose reasoning Bauer's was based, Marx did not see the state as the embodiment of the highest morality. Neither Christian nor Jew would be free until the bourgeois state was dissolved.

At this point, major elements of Marx's philosophy were well structured. He had reversed Hegel's view that ideas change material conditions. In Marx's early journalistic efforts, the intervention of Feuerbach resulted in a conversion of Hegel's idealism to materialism or realism. Marx did retain his Hegelian belief in rationality, which was in turn derived from Kant and the *philosophes* of the French Revolution.

Marx's radical attack on the state estranged him from Ruge, thus temporarily ending Marx's journalistic career. The ensuing hiatus created by his unemployment gave him the opportunity to study communism and socialism in Paris. With its radical heritage from the French Revolution, Paris was the only continental city with a sophisticated intellectual tradition.

Further Intellectual Development

Marx lived in Paris only from 1843 to 1845, but his stay was extraordinarily productive. He completed his economic and philosophical studies and became acquainted with Heinrich Heine, Pierre Proudhon, and Frederick Engels, and by the end of 1844 had become a communist. In addition to his journalism, he produced what is now published as the *Economic and Philosophic Manuscripts of 1844*. Here the philosophic conception of alienation, the concept of man estranged from his true self, was connected to the capitalist economy. The human being as producer is seen as estranged from the product of his labor in that he has to sell his creative capacity to work in order to satisfy physical needs for survival. The only thing he can sell is his labor power. The capitalist purchases this labor power and receives most of the goods it produces. A human being can be restored to his essential (i.e., ideal) self only when private property is eliminated because this alienation is a direct result of private ownership of the means of production. Marx fills out this philosophical vision of the treatise with economic theories.

Pressured by Prussian authorities, François Guizot, leader of the republic in France, forced Marx to leave Paris. In Brussels, where he then moved, Marx wrote the *Theses on Feuerbach* in the spring of 1845 and, in collaboration with Engels, *The German Ideology*. Although neither work was published for many decades, these two works marked the transition from Marx's philosophical pre-occupations to his economic, historical, and sociological work.

The main thrust of his *Theses on Feuerbach* was that the "old" materialism was passive and not dynamic. Philosophy and action, theory and practice, had to be united to change the world. Feuerbach had failed to unite them. In *The German Ideology,* largely a polemic against his former teacher Bruno Bauer and the Young Hegelians, Marx expounded on the materialist conception of history and set the grounds for linking theory and practice. The next step in the critique of capitalism came in *Wage Labor and Capital* (originally lectures given to a German workers' society in Brussels). The relationship between capital and labor later became central both to his *Contribution to the Critique of Political Economy,* published in 1859, and to volume 1 of *Capital,* his masterpiece, which was published in 1867.

Pierre Proudhon (1809-65)

In 1847, Marx wrote *Poverty of Philosophy* as an answer to Pierre Proudhon's *Systems of Contradictions or the Philosophy of Poverty,* written in 1846. Proudhon thereby became the first of the three major figures of the nineteenth century with whom Marx became engaged in mortal combat. The ideas of Pierre Proudhon, Ferdinand Lassalle, and Mikhail Bakunin competed with those of Marx for the minds and hearts of the dispossessed, and each of the three had a significant following in Europe. In France, Proudhon was a hero of the petite bourgeoisie, small farmers, and the proletariat because of his support of those groups during the French Revolution and his insistence that their respective interests were not in conflict.

Proudhon's main ideas had been published in 1840 in his book *What Is Property?* In 1845, Marx had completed but not published *The German Ideology,* in which he had finished with Hegelian idealism. Armed with a thoroughly consistent conception of historical materialism, Marx was ready to take on all nonbelievers. Proudhon was offered no quarter. Marx insisted that all subscribe to his orthodoxy or suffer the pains of his vengeful pen; this stance cost him dearly among those whose support for the workers' movement was needed. Proudhon was but the first.

Proudhon seemed an easy mark. Marx rightly claimed that Proudhon did not understand Hegel, on whose ideas Marx's own theories purported to be built. Proudhon did not read German, so he got his Hegel second-hand. And Marx further claimed that Proudhon's aim, to dissolve *all* institutions (except for a loose federation of some local and possibly regional associations), on the grounds that *all* organizations were coercive, was wildly unrealistic.

Proudhon's panacea for *all* economic ills was the establishment of people's banks, exchange banks that would provide unlimited interest-free credit to businessmen. Because he held a labor theory of value, he would protect workers from exploitation by using the banks as a vehicle to aid the exchange of goods—at their full labor value—between workers. Despite the contention explicit in the title of his earlier book *Property Is Theft,* he did not wish to nationalize private property, including land, for doing so would create a powerful state. He wanted to provide for its "use" (not ownership) by workers, who would gain the income that the property provided. Interest, rent, and profit would thereby disappear. Proudhon had wide appeal among those dispossessed by the industrial revolution, including small farmers and artisans whose position had been undermined by the spread of the factory system in towns and in the countryside, as well as to the industrial proletariat newly arriving on the economic scene.

Marx perceived Poudhon's proposals as preposterous, entirely irrelevant to the problems they were designed to address. In response, Marx wrote *Poverty of Philosophy* with the aim of destroying Proudhon's intellectual reputation. In the event, Marx's book was read by very few and was without influence on Proudhon's standing. Indeed, his following grew year by year. But Marx's unrelenting hostility caused resentment among Proudhon's followers and laid the ground for the bitter battles in the First International (see page 149), which were partly responsible for its destruction.

The Manifesto of the Communist Party

Marx's intellectual ideas were most fully expressed in popular format in the *Manifesto of the Communist Party,* which was published in 1848, on the eve of a series of revolts that shook Europe. Marx was in no way responsible for the revolutions, but the *Manifesto* was a call to arms, a demand for reform, and became the rallying cry for the oppressed of Europe. As Marx had intended, it badly scared the middle and aristocratic classes, and made Marx notorious throughout Europe.

As early as 1836, some radical German workers who lived in Paris formed a secret association called the League of the Just, which by 1842 had become the Communist League. The Communist League asked Marx and Engels to draw up a manifesto; Engels wrote the first draft, which Marx revised.

In the form that comes down to us, this *Manifesto* became the most widely read and influential document of modern socialism. It was translated and published first in the United States and later in Poland, Russia, Switzerland, Denmark, Germany, and Italy. Although aimed at the industrial workers of

Europe, there were few such workers outside England and France. Seemingly revolutionary in its call for the overthrow of capitalism, the *Manifesto* is basically a statement of Marx's theories of the class struggle and a celebration of the capacity of capitalism to revolutionize the world through industrial progress and the extension of the market. It is also a call for the unity of all socialist parties to fight against oppression and prepare for revolutionary change.

The specific policy measures recommended reflect the prevailing tone of contemporary agitation. The *Manifesto* demands a graduated income tax, the removal of all rights to inheritance, a central bank, centralized communication and transportation systems, the cultivation of waste lands, free public education, and abolition of child labor, most of which would appeal to the bourgeoisie, who had been agitating for some of these reforms anyway. Astutely, Marx did not call for the nationalization of land. Such a call would have antagonized large sections of the bourgeoisie and farming community, whose support for the revolution was necessary. Published in multiple editions over the years, the text nevertheless became the political bible for Marxist revolutionaries.

From 1848 to 1849, Marx was in Cologne and edited the *Neue Rheinische Zeitung*. Although Marx was hardly responsible for the revolutions of those years, the authorities in Cologne charged him with "press offenses" and incitement to revolution. In fact, when the revolutions in Europe were either suppressed or had evaporated because of their followers' lack of conviction, the *Neue Rheinische Zeitung* became most militant. Its readership increased, and it was viewed by the authorities as increasingly dangerous. Although the counterrevolution was firmly established, Marx wrote fiery articles that panicked subscribers and caused the paper to lose money. When the government in Paris dissolved the democratic assembly that had declared all taxes illegal, Marx urged people to resist attempts to collect taxes. In consequence, the newspaper was suppressed, and Marx was arrested for sedition.

The incident that precipitated his arrest was a bitter four-day battle in Paris that ended the revolution in June 1848. (That last-ditch attempt to save the revolution appears to have been instigated by Auguste Blanqui, a wildly radical revolutionary who was in jail at the time.) Marx was tried before a jury. He took the opportunity to deliver a lengthy harangue on politics, history, and economics. The jury was so impressed by his polemics that it not only declared him innocent of all charges but thanked him for an instructive and interesting address from which they had all greatly profited.

Not long afterward, England allowed Marx to immigrate. He and his family arrived in London on 24 August 1849; they were followed a month later by Engels. From abroad, Marx continued to promulgate the view that the European revolution would break out once again, and for a time he continued his agitation against the conservative French Republic.

CHAPTER 14

MARX IN ENGLAND

The second half of Marx's life was spent in England. He was thirty-one years old when he arrived there with his growing family; he spent the next twenty years in abject poverty, and lived off the beneficence of friends. He was also cut off from the mainstream of intellectual life in Britain because the English were not sympathetic to Marxism and were basically uninterested in European affairs. Marx, for his part, was jealous of rivals, disliked English society, and demanded of his adherents not only adulation and flattery but also total submission.

These arrogant demands were made by a revolutionary head of a family of eight living in two rooms in Soho, one of London's worst slums. A Prussian police agent reported on the life of the Marxes on Dean Street: "Marx lives in one of the worst and hence cheapest quarters in London. . . . There is not one piece of good furniture. . . . Everything is broken, tattered and torn, finger-thick dust everywhere, and everything in the greatest disorder; a large, old-fashioned table, covered with waxcloth, stands in the middle of the drawing room, on it lie manuscripts, books, newspapers, then the children's toys, bits and pieces of the women's sewing things, next to it a few teacups with broken rims, dirty spoons, knives, forks, candlesticks, inkpot, glasses, dutch clay pipes, tobacco-ash, in a word all kinds of trash, and everything on one table; a junk dealer would be ashamed of it. When you enter the Marx flat your sight is dimmed by coal and tobacco smoke so that you grope around at first as if you were in a cave. . . . Everything is dirty, everything covered with dust; it is dangerous to sit down. Here is a chair with only three legs, there the children play kitchen on another chair that happens to be whole. . . . This is the faithful portrait of the family life of the communist leader Marx."[1]

Marx was not only poor but was plagued by physical illness exacerbated by overwork, worry, too much smoking, and lack of exercise. He was hardly in a position to develop friends among the English radicals and trade unionists, many of whom were middle-class intellectuals, often smug, and certainly unwilling to learn from a brooding, intemperate foreigner. Marx consorted mainly with German exiles and depended for friendship and finances particularly on Frederick Engels.

Marx had to suffer the further chagrin of seeing romantic patriots such as Ferenc Kossuth and Giuseppe Garibaldi publicly cheered in the London streets. Those figures, Giuseppe Mazzini among them, who spoke for the national aspirations of their countries, without revolutionary ideologies to frighten the wealthy, were not a danger to the status quo in England. In short, they were heroic, picturesque, and harmless.

England was by no means in revolutionary ferment. The Chartist Movement was a workers' (though not a trade unionists') movement to secure industrial emancipation through the extension of political rights, electoral reform, and suffrage. In the 1830s and 1840s, the Chartists, nonsocialist and nonrevolutionary, pressed hard but nonviolently for their goals, and were viewed by Marx as an unlikely collection of romantics, reformers, philosophical radicals, dispossessed farmers, and artisans without program or direction. Chartism developed as a consequence of the declining fortunes of the lower middle class, which accompanied rapid economic growth favorable to industrialists and bankers but not yet to the middle class. The economic growth of England was carried on the backs of peasants, artisans, and workers. Chartism vanished by the end of the 1850s in the wake of an economic boom, the first to be recognized in European history, which alleviated much of the misery of those affected by the hungry 1840s and 1850s.

There was no revolution in sight in England, and Marx recognized this. It was a time for him to reconsider the events of 1848–49: the abortive alliance between the proletariat and the bourgeoisie, for example. The bourgeoisie preferred to protect their property, such as it was, in a society dominated by landlords, financiers, and big businessmen, rather than face an uncertain future in a society without private property. The bourgeois defection from an alliance with the proletariat forced Marx to recognize that alliances with the bourgeoisie were self-defeating, and he spent the rest of his life inveighing against them. Another consideration was whether the proletarian revolution should be led by an elite of professional revolutionaries, who by means of a coup d'état would control the government, train the masses, and rule in their name. Power would then be returned to an enlightened populace free of all class distinction. Or, as industrial capitalism matured, should revolution await the slow development of proletarian class consciousness as it grew in the womb of the bourgeoisie?

Marx believed that failure of the revolution in any country in Europe during the years 1848 to 1849 showed, if anything, that the immaturity of the proletariat proved that a truly classless society had to await the fullness of history. That consideration weighed against premature revolution, with its senseless loss of life and certainty of defeat. Some of his most vitriolic polemics were directed at people such as Wilhelm Weitling, Auguste Blanqui, and Mikhail Bakunin for their recklessness and lack of historical perspective.

In the 1850s, despite the squalor in which he lived, the deaths of three of his children, the indignity of hiding from creditors, the regular pawning of his clothes, and near starvation, Marx visited the British Museum almost daily. He worked long hours, going to bed only at two or three in the morning. He continued his analysis of capitalism and wrote several books alone and with Engels. He also contributed on an irregular basis to the *New York Daily Tribune*. The *Tribune* paid him £1 per article, and when Marx was sick, Engels often wrote the articles for him, including many of the articles on military affairs, about which Engels was an expert. In all, between them both, 487 articles were contributed to the *Tribune*.

During this time, Marx formulated the generalization that only an economic slump could lead to a revolution. But the economic crisis of 1857, which was worldwide, did not have the results he anticipated. Nevertheless, both Marx and Engels continued to watch closely the relationship between the business cycle and revolutionary agitation.

Ferdinand Lassalle

In the course of these years of poverty and readjustment, Marx became entangled with Ferdinand Lassalle (1825-64), the creator of the German Social Democratic movement. Lassalle was a lawyer, a revolutionary, and an extremely intelligent, energetic and wholly self-confident man. But, being of Jewish origin, he knew that many careers were closed to him. Imprisoned for his outspoken criticism of the German government, he recanted his beliefs in public, retrieved his reputation, and with brilliant success organized a political party in Germany. Lassalle differed from Marx in that he did not see state and society as discrete entities and therefore did not see the state as an executive committee of the ruling class. He thought that workers could enter into an alliance with the Prussian king and establish an authoritarian collectivist state headed by the king, which would then be ruled in the interest of the working classes.

Marx admired Lassalle's capacity for organization but distrusted him, thinking him superficial and his ideas intemperate, undisciplined, and without adequate theoretical foundation. Lassalle, for example, continually attempted to make agreements with Otto von Bismarck, whom Marx considered the enemy. Lassalle also went on highly publicized lecture tours, during which his fiery speeches aroused enthusiasm that raised expectations perhaps beyond reasonable levels. He did, however, succeed in forming a widely based political party, rather than small, tightly organized, elite secret cells. Most important, he organized for negotiation, not revolution. He was willing to make alliances with nonbourgeois parties; his nationalism was confined to Germany. One of his programs was to set up workers' cooperatives that were to be organized and financed by the state.

Lassalle's romantic patriotism, his vision of himself as the leader, his support of the petite bourgeoisie as well as the proletariat, were all thought by Marx to be wrongheaded, dangerous, indeed megalomaniacal failings. In any event, Marx could tolerate no rival. Despite Lassalle's success at organizing a viable working-class party, Marx never trusted him. Still, when Lassalle died ingloriously in a duel arising from a trivial love affair, Marx was depressed, if not surprised that such an undisciplined person should come to an untimely and bizarre end. Their differences notwithstanding, Marx recognized that of all the European revolutionaries, Lassalle and he had the most in common by intellectual heritage and conviction.

By the end of the 1850s, aside from the publication of his *Critique of Political Economy* (1859), which was not widely read, Marx was in eclipse, cut off from his natural environment in Europe, living in poverty, squabbling with exiles in London and imprudent revolutionaries on the Continent. It seemed likely that, at only forty-two, he was doomed to obscurity. In the last twenty years of his life, however, Marx's fame grew, as did his notoriety. By the time of his death in 1883 he had become a legend. And indeed, since his death, the Russian Revolution, which provided a political expression for Marx's ideology everywhere in the world, has assured his immortality.

In the 1860s Marx continued to live in poverty. He was no longer engaged by the *New York Daily Tribune* as an occasional contributor. Although Engels's support continued, it was sporadic and insufficient, but a trickle of funds from supporters in Europe helped sustain him. Marx appears to have earned very little from his voluminous writings, much of which went ignored during his lifetime. But he persisted nevertheless. When funds did become available from time to time from various inheritances, he dissipated them. Part of his money went to maintaining appearances, part to excessively costly rents. Marx even speculated on the London Stock Exchange, much to his regret. In short, he was incapable of managing his financial affairs.[2]

His major literary efforts of the 1860s were the writing of *Theories of Surplus Value* (which is often called volume 4 of *Capital*) and the publication of volume 1 of *Capital* in 1867. Volume 1 is by far the most important of the three volumes of *Capital,* because it lays out with powerful clarity all the essentials of Marx's critique of capitalism. Volumes 2 and 3 were completed between 1867 and 1880, but were not published until after Marx's death.

The First International

Marx returned to prominence through the founding of the First International (more formally referred to as the International Working Men's Association) in 1864. The First International began as a consequence of the great International Exposition held in London in 1862, which was a celebration of capitalism with its new technical marvels and accompanying vast growth of wealth. Louis Napoleon, anxious to impress French workers with the benefits of capitalism — and to undermine Proudhon, whose views still held sway over French workers — sent a delegation of artisans to the exhibition.

Business firms in Prussia and other parts of Germany also dispatched working-class delegates to London to attend the International Exposition. These European delegations met with British trade unionists, who had until that time ignored politics in favor of business unionism. But the British capitalists had been importing "blacklegs" (strikebreakers) from Europe, and British workers were anxious to enlist the aid of fellow workers in Europe to prevent this practice.

With the development of capitalism and liberalism, the feudal grip was loosening all over Europe, even in czarist Russia. The needs of capitalism and the demands for liberty were moving rapidly together, creating a degree of common interest between the bourgeoisie, workers, and peasants.

There had been an uprising in Poland in 1863, which was crushed by Prussian soldiers. London workers drafted a manifesto in support of the Poles and Marx attended a mass meeting held in St. James Hall in their honor. He normally avoided such meetings, but saw political opportunities in this one. He took full advantage of this opportunity to establish himself as the leader of the International and presented the audience with *An Address to the Working Classes,* a retrospective of what had happened to the working class since 1845. The essential message of his address was that, despite the enormous increase in trade in the last twenty years and the growth of taxable income and wealth, the benefits were entirely confined to the propertied classes. He spoke of poverty, of starvation, and of the growth of misery in a period of apparent prosperity. He spoke of the enormous migrations to America as people fled insufferable conditions. The only good news he had to report was the passage of the Ten Hours Bill after thirty years of struggle and the Rochdale pioneers, a development of the Cooperative Movement in England. (From that movement evolved the present British Labour party.) He emphasized that the working class had to become sophisticated about international affairs because those affairs affected them immediately. Workers of the world needed to unite in support of their common interests.

One of Marx's conclusions based on the events of 1848-49 was the necessity for an open and broad-based proletarian movement rather than secret cells that clandestinely propagandized workers. The First International was a realization of this idea, but those who became members had very mixed goals and ideologies. They included Owenist Utopians and Chartists, both relics of an earlier day; individualists; and British trade unionists such as the Christian Socialists, who were opposed to political activity of any kind. The English members were thoroughly divided among themselves. From France there were Fourierists and Cabetists—also relics. There were also numerous supporters of Louis Blanc who were certainly not socialists but held quirky ideas about national workshops, and there were Blanquists who were anxious to instigate uprisings whenever possible. The strongest group from France were the Proudhonists, who wished to rid the world of capitalism by setting up people's banks. There were also German Utopians such as Wilhelm Weitling, who had been active during 1848. And finally there was the General Union of German Workers, founded by Lassalle and still very popular in Germany. All attended the London conference: socialists and nonsocialists, activists, utopians, and mad revolutionaries—a dangerous mixture that Marx was attempting to weld into an effective international organization speaking and acting on behalf of the European proletariat.

For a number of years, Marx was the uncontested leader of this conglomeration, forming policy with an iron hand, throwing all his strength into the International's development. He was enormously successful. The only important organization that did not finally join the International was the Lassallist German party. After Lassalle's death, the leadership had been taken by J.B. von Schweitzer, a dedicated Marxist, on whom all Marx's dislike and jealousy of Lassalle nevertheless devolved. Aside from doctrinal differences with the Lassalleans, Marx could not countenance a powerful, well-led, independent-minded group outside of his authority. Consequently, Marx refused to countenance any connection between von Schweitzer's organization and the International.

During the time that Marx was building the International, his personal affairs were in increasingly desperate straits. Not only was he without any source of income and wholly dependent on Engels, but Jenny Marx was sick. Marx himself suffered from a liver ailment and very painful boils all over his body; he could not afford sustained medical treatment and slept little. (Marx remarked that his afflictions could be better borne by a "good" Christian, who would be better able to turn his suffering to good account.) The misery of his personal life left its mark on his intolerant personality, on his relations with most of his supporters and rivals, and on his work. These were also the years when he was working on the first volume of *Capital*. Finally, Marx had to drop everything and go to a seaside resort (with funds supplied by Engels) to recover his health.

Mikhail Bakunin

The battle between Marx and Mikhail Bakunin (1814-76) typifies the ambiguities within the International that ultimately led to its dissolution. Although each unit of the International had a national base and programs of its own, the organization spoke publicly through the voice of Marx. The struggle among the units to have their separate voices and causes enunciated was unending.

Marx erroneously believed that he could weld disparate groups of dissatisfied workers and middle-class intellectuals with vastly differing interests and world views into a cohesive world power speaking with a single voice in the interest of the "masses." Marx accepted that his alliance with the middle classes was a tactic to be used for short-run advantage, but what he did not realize, ever, was the force of nationalism. He believed that the interests of the proletariat transcended national borders and that the proletariat would rise above them.

Marx's hostility to nationalism might have made Bakunin, the anarchist, a natural ally. But Bakunin's central theory was that the goal of agitation was to remove all restraints on human activity. Marx's views, he believed, were "authoritarian communism." The thrust of Bakunin's anarchism was antinationalist and so radically individualistic that Marx thought its achievement unlikely.

The dispute was practical as well as theoretical. Bakunin opposed all alliances with bourgeois political parties. Although Marx had come to the same conclusion in consequence of the failure of alliances in 1848, he held that the time was not ripe for the proletariat to go it alone. The ideological differences separating the two revolutionists were stated by Bakunin: "We, revolutionary anarchists, are the enemies of all forms of state and state organization . . . we think that all state rule, all government, being by their very nature placed outside the mass of people, must necessarily seek to be subjected to customs and purposes entirely foreign to [them]. We therefore declare ourselves to be foes . . . of all state organizations as such, and believe that the people can only be happy and free, when, organized from below by means of [their] own autonomy and completely free associations, without the supervision of any guardians, [they] will create [their] own life. We believe power corrupts those who wield it as much as those who are forced to obey it."

The dispute with Bakunin was a major cause of Marx's decision to dissolve the First International. It was not the only cause. But at the Congress in the Hague, in 1872, Marx succeeded in having Bakunin and his organization expelled. Even his ultimate defeat of Bakunin could not bring about the unity of purpose that he sought.

Marx, seeing the International dissolving before him, moved it to New York, where it died a year later. The precipitating cause of the decline of the First International was the loss of interest in revolutionary activity by the British. Indeed, all European groups were losing interest. During the late 1860s, prosperity and the general weakening of anticombination laws in England reduced trade union militancy. And the British were never Marxist to begin with. Like people in all national movements, they saw their problems in terms of their country's conditions. It is likely that even in the absence of the events of the Franco-Prussian War and the Paris Commune, the International would have broken up.

To summarize, the elements that led to the destruction of the First International were, in probable order of importance, the withdrawal of British support; widely differing national interests and programs in Europe; Marx's inability to control "sects," as he called them, with vastly differing perspectives; and the International's terrorist reputation, which caused a mass defection, not simply by the bourgeois contingent but by many of Marx's supporters as well.

The Franco-Prussian War and the Paris Commune

Worker concern with national rather than international conditions sorely tested the strength of working-class solidarity during the Franco-Prussian War of 1870. Nationalism superseded working-class unity in France and Germany in 1870 as workers flocked to the colors. Marx originally supported the German cause, hoping for greater German unification and with it the chances for a consolidated and powerful working class. However, the French army was quickly defeated at Sedan, the emperor was taken prisoner, and Paris was besieged. Bismarck annexed Alsace-Lorraine and levied an indemnity of 5 billion francs on France. These events, plus accounts of atrocities, turned Marx and the British public sharply against the Germans.

To Marx's delight, the Lassalleans in the German Reichstag voted against credits to carry on the war. This was the first time the working class had acted in class interest rather than national interest.

After the defeat at Sedan and the capture of the emperor, a vacuum of power existed in Paris. The Prussians were at the gates, but did not try to enter. Louis Thiers, president of the newly declared Republic of France, withdrew all officials to Versailles, leaving only the Central Committee of the National Guard in command in Paris. The National Guard, a volunteer civilian force with radical sympathies, granted voting rights to all males. They held an election in March 1871, creating an assembly known as the Paris Commune.

Thiers's provisional government became alarmed and tried to take over the government of Paris by disarming the National Guard. The refusal of the National Guard to give up their arms precipitated civil war between the French government and the Paris Commune.

The Commune was not organized at the instigation of Marx, nor was it Marxist in character. Although run by a dictatorship, its makeup was highly heterogeneous, comprising followers of Blanqui, Proudhon, Bakunin, and patriots simply fighting for France. Support for the Commune came from workers, soldiers, writers, various politicians, foreign exiles, liberals, bohemians, and adventurers—who had in common a hatred of priests, Prussians, Bonapartists, and Orleanist reactionaries. Thiers and his ministers were seen as representing the generals, financiers, and priests.

Thiers tried to raise an army to liberate Paris from the Commune, but he was unable to do so until Bismarck, once peace was made, released the captive French army into the hands of the Versailles government. The communards, unable to hold out long against the army of Versailles, killed some hostages, including the archbishop of Paris. These relatively few murders and some minor acts of incendiarism were exaggerated. The Versailles officials propagandized the alleged atrocities worldwide, and the revenge of the army was merciless. The communards were massacred without regard to age and sex or involvement in the Commune, and deaths exceeded twenty thousand.

Marx's most famous polemic, *The Civil War in France,* was an address to the General Council of the First International. It argued that the Commune had provided the first important example of class warfare undertaken by the proletariat. The force of his address, despite its patently flawed analysis, made the International so notorious that many people believed Marxists were responsible for the atrocities that Thiers had attributed to them.

In his printed address, Marx described the conditions leading up to the Commune, its organization, and its demise. His purpose was to show, first, the contrast between the beneficial effects of the Commune and the repressive nature of the centrally controlled empire and republic. He wanted to highlight the contrast between corruption of the empire and the self-sacrifice and idealism of the workers. His second purpose was to provide a blueprint for a communist revolution. The program of the Commune was not Marxist, however, and there was little relationship between its actions and what Marx had called for in the *Manifesto* and elsewhere.

In the third part of his address, Marx outlined the political organization of the Commune, both actual and potential. The model called for decentralization into communes of the great industrial centers of France. However, the nation would remain unified through a plan, about which Marx was not wholly clear, to relate the communes to the central government.

Marx's pamphlet sold well and contributed to the decline of the International. Marx was widely seen as supporting what appeared to be terrorism and barbarism. For one thing, he had struck at the base of private property, which most of the members of the International were not ready to concede was evil. And certainly the program of the Commune was not universally acceptable. Others had sown the wind; Marx reaped the whirlwind.

What Marx gained in notoriety from his pamphlet, he lost in support for the workingman's cause. If Marx appeared to accept the death of some of the hostages by the Commune with equanimity, the revenge of the Versailles government on the communards proved all his charges against it. In *The Civil War in France,* Marx had called the Commune the first important example of class warfare to be taken by the proletariat. Nevertheless, the Commune was organized in violation of Marx's principles, adhering more closely to those of Proudhon and Blanqui, whom Marx spent his life fighting. It also vastly exaggerated the role of the working class. Marx's address embarrassed many members of the International and certainly hastened its dissolution. And Marx's reputation as a terrorist followed him thereafter. He was known as the Red Terrorist Doctor, was the target of threatening letters, was shadowed by the police, and was followed by crowds in the streets. But Marx, dismissing all criticism, reveled in the publicity and appeared not to realize how much damage he had done.

Last Years, Last Works

By 1870, Engels had sold his interest in the firm of Erman and Engels and had moved to London. Thereafter he was able to support Marx and his family; the terrible hardships of the 1850s and 1860s were never repeated.

These later years should have been good ones for the Marx family. But two of Marx's daughters, Jenny and Laura, married Frenchmen; neither marriage was wholly approved by Marx, and although both were revolutionaries, they proved to be poor husbands. Eleanor (Tussy), the youngest daughter, was unable to pursue her chosen stage career until after the death of her parents, who disapproved. She ultimately married Edward Averling, an Englishman who was also interested in the stage. At the time of Marx's death, in 1883, Eleanor was twenty-eight. She committed suicide at age forty-two.

The last years of Marx's life were fully occupied. Although he thought of himself as old, he was only fifty-two in 1870, and his declining health was buoyed by periodic visits to Karlsbad, a reduced work load, long walks, and proper medical attention. Yet from 1870 onward, his health steadily deteriorated.

Meanwhile, the autonomy of political parties in Europe was growing, and Marx's influence was declining. In Germany there were two parties, roughly proletarian in outlook: the Eisenach party and the followers of Lassalle. Both were successful at the polls and met to unite at Gotha in May 1875 to form the Social Democratic party that now exists in Germany.

Marx's last important intellectual contribution to Marxism appears in the *Critique of the Gotha Programme*. The *Critique,* which consisted of marginal notes to the text of the program itself, shed some light on Marx's view of a communist society (see chapter 11).

The fact of the matter is that in addition to being read by very few people, Marx's *Critique* never even reached the assemblage at Gotha. Marx and Engels were thought to be out of touch with the realities of the German situation and were simply ignored. Not until 1891, eight years after Marx's death, did this important theoretical statement come to public light.

After 1875, Marx turned his attention to Russia and Turkey, going so far as to learn the languages of both countries. Although for most of his life he had dismissed the possibility of revolution in Russia, he became more optimistic in these later years. He was greatly encouraged by the intelligence of the Russian Marxists and their dedication to revolution. He also appeared to approve of the terrorist tactics of some of the revolutionaries, on the grounds that in a totally repressed society, only secret societies can survive. Terror was the only practical weapon. Marx hoped that Russian wars with Turkey would lead to a revolution within Russia, the most backward and despotic country in Europe, which would spread to the rest of Europe. On the question whether socialism could develop in Russia, a mainly agricultural country, from a revolutionary program of communal ownership of land, thus bypassing a capitalist stage, Marx was equivocal.

Marx's followers in Europe were not Marxist purists. Their thinking included elements of all the major heresies against which Marx had fought so long and hard. Even Marx's sons-in-law were tainted with Proudhonism and Bakuninism. All of which prompted Marx's famous remark, "What is certain is that I am no Marxist."

By the end of 1881 it was clear that Jenny Marx was dying. Marx himself had been in bed with bronchitis for two months, but kept the death watch along with "Lenchen" (Helene Demuth). When Jenny died, on 2 December 1881, her ailing husband was forbidden by the doctor to attend the funeral.

Following his wife's death, Marx went to France to stay with daughter Jenny Longuet and her children. Charles Longuet was too busy with French politics to help his wife, who was about to have their fourth child. Shortly after the birth, when Marx returned to England, Jenny fell sick with what was probably bladder cancer and died 11 January 1883. Marx was stricken with grief by the news of the death of his first-born, and two months later Marx himself was dead. He had developed a lung abscess and on 14 March died in his sleep while seated in an armchair. With only a few people in attendance, he was buried in Highgate Cemetery next to his wife. In 1956 a socialist workers' organization placed a large marble monument on the grave.

Engels survived until 1895, in his final years the revered head of the socialist movement. Amiable and good-natured to the end, he worked in the socialist cause, editing Marx's papers and clarifying (and simplifying) their meaning in innumerable letters. He took part in the founding of the Second International in 1889 and published two entirely new works, *The Origin of the Family, Private Property and the State* (1884) and *Ludwig Feuerbach and the End of the Classical German Philosophy* (1886).

CHRONOLOGY OF EVENTS
IN MARX'S LIFE

1818   Karl Marx born 5 May in Trier, Prussia, now part of West Germany.

1820   Frederick Engels born 28 November at Barmen, now in West Germany.

1830-35 Marx studies at Frederick William High School in Trier.

1835   Spends one year at the University of Bonn, Faculty of Law. Engaged to Jenny von Westphalen.

1836-41 Studies law, history, and philosophy at Berlin University. Joins Young Hegelians.

1838   Marx's father dies.

1841   Marx receives degree from Jena University.

1842   Baron von Westphalen, his friend and later father-in-law, dies. Marx becomes editor of the *Rheinische Zeitung* and collaborates with Arnold Ruge.

1843   Marx marries Jenny von Westphalen. Studies French Socialism. Writes *Critique of Hegel's Philosophy of Right,* and writes *On the Jewish Question* in response to Bruno Bauer.

1844   Writes *Economic and Philosophical Manuscripts of 1844* and *The Holy Family.* Meets Heinrich Heine, Proudhon, and Engels. Daughter Jenny is born. Engels makes a contribution to a double issue of the *Deutsche-Französische Jahrbücher* and his collaboration with Marx begins.

1845   Marx is banished from Paris by Guizot under pressure from the Prussians and moves to Brussels. Writes *Theses on Feuerbach*. Begins *The German Ideology* with Engels. Daughter Laura is born. Is forced to renounce Prussian citizenship, which he never regains.

1846   Son Edgar is born. *The German Ideology* is completed, but not published. Becomes active in revolutionary politics.

1847   Writes *The Poverty of Philosophy* on Proudhon. Joins the Communist League. Lectures on "Protection, Free Trade, Wage Labor and Capital." Begins drafting *The Communist Manifesto*. Meets, discusses, and fights with Wilhelm Weitling, a German communist leader.

1848   Publishes *The Communist Manifesto*. Is expelled from Brussels. Reorganizes the Communist League. Writes articles for *Neue Rheinische Zeitung*.

1849   Continues writing for the *Neue Rheinische Zeitung*. Publishes *Wage Labor and Capital*. Is acquitted by a jury in Cologne of press offenses and incitement to armed insurrection. Is expelled from Cologne. *Neue Rheinische Zeitung* is suppressed. Is again expelled from Paris. Son Guido is born. Leaves Paris for permanent exile in London.

1850   Addresses the Central Committee of the Communist League. Writes articles for the *Neue Rheinische Zeitung* and writes the *Class Struggles in France*. Guido Marx dies. Lectures to the Workers Educational League in London.

1851   Daughter Franziska is born. Frederick Demuth, the illegitimate son of Helene Demuth and Karl Marx, is born. Lives in poverty on Dean Street in Soho, London. Contributes to the *New York Daily Tribune*.

1852   Franziska Marx dies. Contributes to numerous newspapers. The Communist League is dissolved. Bickers ceaselessly with German émigrés. Writes *The Eighteenth Brumaire of Louis Bonaparte*.

1853   The Cologne Communist Trial. Writes on Lord Palmerston.

1855   Writes articles for the *Neue Oder Zeitung*. Edgar Marx dies. Daughter Eleanor is born.

1856   Writes *Diplomatic History of Eighteenth Century.*

1857-58 Writes the *Grundrisse* (Outlines of a *Critique of Political Economy*)
         Writes articles for the *New American Encyclopedia.* Begins corres-
         pondence with Lassalle.

1859   Publishes the *Critique of Political Economy* and the Preface to a *Cri-
         tique of Political Economy.*

1860   Writes a polemic entitled *Herr Vogt.*

1861-62 Makes contributions to *Die Presse* in Vienna. Meets with Lassalle
         in Berlin.

1862   Writes *Theories of Surplus Value* and *The Polish Question.*

1863   Starts writing volume 2 of *Capital,* which takes 14 years to complete.

1864   Lassalle dies. The First International is founded in St. Martin's Hall,
         London; Marx writes the Inaugural Address. Begins writing *Capital,*
         volume 3.

1865   Lectures on "Value, Price, and Profit."

1866   First Congress of International is held in Vienna.

1867   Volume 1 of *Capital* is published. Second Congress of the Interna-
         tional is held in Lausanne.

1868   The Third Congress of the International is held in Brussels. Mikhail
         Bakunin founds International Alliance of Socialist Democracy. Marx's
         fight with Bakunin is under way. Laura Marx, daughter, marries Paul
         LaFargue.

1869   The Social Democratic party is founded in Germany. Engels retires
         from business. Marx's financial woes are at an end. The Fourth Con-
         gress of the International is held in Basel.

1870   Engels moves to London. The Franco-Prussian War begins and ends.
         Marx continues to work on volumes 2 and 3 of *Capital.*

1871   Writes *The Civil War in France*. After the events of the Paris Commune, the Second Conference of the International is held in London.

1872   Bakunin is expelled from the International. The General Council of the International is moved to New York City. Jenny Marx marries Charles Longuet.

1873   The preface to the second German edition of *Capital*, volume 1, is published. Writes pamphlet against Bakunin. Is seriously ill.

1874   Goes to Karlsbad for a cure.

1875   German workers' parties unite in Gotha. Marx writes a *Critique of the Gotha Programme*, which is not heard by the delegates. Moves to Maitland Park Road to live in some comfort.

1876   Bakunin dies. Marx returns to Karlsbad for his health.

1877   Collaborates with Engels in writing *Anti-Dühring*. Marx goes to Neuenahr for his health.

1878   Antisocialist laws in Germany prevent Marx from returning to Karlsbad.

1881   Jenny Marx dies.

1882   Preface to the second Russian edition of *The Communist Manifesto* is published. Marx seeks to recover in Algiers but to no avail.

1883   Daughter Jenny Longuet dies in January. Marx dies in March.

1885   *Capital*, volume 2, is published.

1894   *Capital*, volume 3, is published.

1895   Frederick Engels dies.

NOTES

PREFACE (pp. ix-xii)

1. Frederick Engels, speech at the graveside of Karl Marx, delivered 17 March 1883, in *Marx, Engels Selected Works* (Moscow: Foreign Languages Publishing House, 1958), 2:167. Hereafter cited as *MESW*.

CHAPTER 1. Introduction (pp. 1-8)

1. Karl Marx and Frederick Engels, *The German Ideology* (New York: International Publishers, 1939).

CHAPTER 2. Hegel and Feuerbach (pp. 9-17)

1. Frederick Engels, *Ludwig Feuerbach and the End of Classical German Philosophy, MESW,* 2:369.
    2. Ibid., 372-73.
    3. Ibid., 367.
    4. Ibid., 367-68.
    5. Ibid., 373.
    6. Ibid.
    7. Ibid., 378.
    8. Ibid., 381.
    9. Ibid., 382.
    10. Ibid.
    11. Ibid.
    12. Ibid., 383-84.
    13. Ibid., 384.
    14. Ibid., 386.
    15. Ibid., 387-88.
    16. Karl Marx, *Theses on Feuerbach, MESW,* 403-5.

CHAPTER 3. The Theory of Alienation (pp. 19-28)

1. Karl Marx, "Critique of the Hegelian Dialectic and Philosophy as a Whole," *Economic and Philosophic Manuscripts of 1844* (Moscow: Foreign Languages Publishing House, 1961), 152.
2. Ibid., 162-63.
3. Ibid., 166.
4. Karl Marx and Frederick Engels, *The Holy Family or Critique of Critical Critiques* (Chicago: Charles H. Kerr, 1904), 113-16.
5. Karl Marx, *Capital: A Critique of Political Economy* (Chicago: Charles H. Kerr, 1906), 1:25.
6. Marx, *Economic and Philosophic Manuscripts of 1844*, 69.
7. Ibid., 70.
8. Ibid., 72.
9. Ibid., 133.
10. Ibid.
11. Ibid., 89.

CHAPTER 4. Economic Systems Prior to Capitalism (pp. 29-39)

1. Karl Marx, *Pre-Capitalist Economic Formations,* ed. E.J. Hobsbawm (New York: International Publishers, 1964).
2. Ibid., 104.
3. Ibid., 111.
4. Ibid., 109.
5. Ibid., 84.
6. Ibid., 92.
7. Ibid., 93.
8. Ibid.
9. Ibid., 105.
10. Ibid., 112.
11. Ibid., 113-16.
12. Ibid., 118.

CHAPTER 5. Scientific Socialism, Socialism, and Anarchism (pp. 41-52)

1. Marx and Engels, *The German Ideology.*
2. Ibid., 83.
3. Ibid.
4. Ibid., 85.

5. Frederick Engels, *Socialism, Utopian and Scientific, MESW,* 2:117.

6. Ibid., 122.

7. Ibid., 123.

8. Ibid., 124.

9. Ibid.

10. Ibid.

11. Ibid., 126.

12. Ibid., 127.

13. Ibid., 128.

14. Frederick Engels, "On the Occasion of Karl Marx's Death," written 12 May 1883. Published in *Der Sozialdemocrat,* no. 21, 17 May 1883, reprinted in Marx, Engels, Lenin, *Anarchism and Anarcho-Syndicalism* (Moscow: Progress Publishers, 1972), 171.

15. Isaiah Berlin, *Karl Marx, His Life and Environment,* Home University Library, 2d ed. (London: Oxford University Press, 1984), 130.

16. Quoted in Paul Thomas, *Karl Marx and the Anarchists* (London: Routledge and Kegan Paul, 1980), 174.

CHAPTER 6. The Materialist Conception of History (pp. 53-62)

1. Marx and Engels, *The German Ideology,* 6-7.

2. Ibid.

3. Marx, *Preface to the Critique of Political Economy, MESW,* 1:363.

4. Marx and Engels, *The German Ideology,* 6-7.

5. Ibid.

6. Ibid., 10.

7. Ibid., 13.

8. Ibid.

9. Ibid., 14.

10. Engels, *Ludwig Feuerbach, MESW,* 2:394.

11. Ibid.

12. Ibid.

13. Ibid.

14. Ibid., 394-95.

15. Ibid., 395.

16. Engels, Letter to J. Block, 21 and 22 September 1890, "Selected Correspondence," *MESW,* 2:488.

17. Ibid.

18. Ibid.

19. Ibid., 490

20. *Capital,* 1:81-84.
21. Engels, *Ludwig Feuerbach, MESW,* 2:377.

CHAPTER 7. The Economic Interpretation of History—Classes
(pp. 63-71)

1. Engels, *Anti-Dühring* (Moscow: Foreign Languages Publishing House, 1954), 203.
2. Ibid.
3. Ibid., 204.
4. Ibid., 209.
5. Marx, *The Poverty of Philosophy* (Chicago: Charles H. Kerr, 1909), 136-37.
6. Ibid., 137.
7. Marx and Engels, *Manifesto of the Communist Party, MESW,* 1:35.
8. Ibid., 36.
9. Ibid.
10. Ibid.
11. Ibid., 37.
12. Ibid., 38.
13. Ibid.
14. Ibid., 39.
15. Ibid., 40.
16. Ibid., 45.

CHAPTER 8. The Superstructure (pp. 73-80)

1. Engels, *The Origin of the Family, MESW,* 2:253.
2. Marx and Engels, *The German Ideology,* 59.
3. Engels, *Ludwig Feuerbach, MESW,* 2:397.
4. Engels, *Anti-Dühring,* 440.
5. Ibid.
6. Ibid.
7. Marx and Engels, "Toward the Criticism of Hegel's Philosophy of Right," *Deutsche-Französische Jahrbücher* (1843), 378-79.
8. Ibid.
9. Engels, *The Origin of the Family, MESW,* 2:240.
10. Marx, *A World Without Jews* (New York: Philosophical Library, 1959), 9
11 Ibid., 34

CHAPTER 9. Capitalism: Value and Price (pp. 81-94)

1. Marx, *Capital,* 1:44.
2. Ibid., 115.
3. Ibid., 218-19.
4. Ibid., 120.
5. Ibid., 189-90.
6. Ibid., 212.
7. Ibid., 431-32.
8. Ibid., 445.
9. Ibid., 449.
10. Ibid., 681.
11. Ibid., 681-82.
12. Ibid., 3:249.
13. Ibid., 260-61.
14. Ibid., 190.
15. Ibid., 203.
16. Ibid., 208.
17. Ibid., 209-10.
18. Ibid., 212.
19. Ibid.

CHAPTER 10. Capitalism: Crises and Breakdown (pp. 95-109)

1. Marx, *Capital,* 1:649.
2. Ibid.
3. Ibid., 651.
4. Marx, *A Critique of the Gotha Programme, MESW,* 2:281.
5. Marx, *Capital,* 3:309.
6. Ibid., 310.
7. Ibid.
8. Ibid., 1:836-37.
9. Ibid., 3:303.
10. Ibid., 2:591-611.
11. D. Harris, "On Marx's Scheme of Reproduction and Accumulation," in *The Economics of Marxism,* ed. M.C. Howard and J. E. King (Harmondsworth, England: Penguin, 1976), 185-202.
12. Ibid.

CHAPTER 11. Communism (pp. 111-24)

1. Marx, *Poverty of Philosophy*, 218.
2. Marx, *Capital*, 3:283.
3. Frederick Engels, "Preface," ibid., 1:32-33.
4. Ibid., 1:824.
5. Marx, Letter to J. Weydemeyer, 5 March 1852, "Selected Correspondence," *MESW*, 2:86.
6. Marx, *Critique of the Gotha Programme*, *MESW*, 2:32-33.
7. Engels, Introduction to *Civil War in France*, *MESW*, 1:484-85
8. Ibid.
9. Marx, Letter to J. Weydemeyer.
10. Marx, *Capital*, 1:90-91.
11. Marx, *Critique of the Gotha Programme*, *MESW*, 2:21-24
12. Marx, *Economic and Philosophic Manuscripts of 1844*, 102
13. Marx, *Capital*, 1:954.
14. Marx and Engels, *The German Ideology*, 22.
15. Engels, *Socialism, Utopian and Scientific*, *MESW*, 2:155.
16. Marx, *Capital*, 3:221.
17. Ibid., 2:412.
18. Engels, *Anti-Dühring*, 407-8.
19. Engels, *Socialism, Utopian and Scientific*, *MESW*, 2:153.
20. Engels, *Anti-Dühring*, 411.
21. Engels, *Socialism, Utopian and Scientific*, *MESW*, 2:149-51.

CHAPTER 12. Evaluation, Summary, and Critique (pp. 125-35)

1. John Schaar, *Escape from Authority* (New York: Harper & Row, 1961)
2. Ibid., 297-98.

CHAPTER 13. Marx as a Young Man (pp. 137-44)

1. The sources of this chapter and chapter 14 are many and various. They include Berlin, *Karl Marx;* David McLellan, *Karl Marx: His Life and Thought* (New York: Harper & Row, 1973); Franz Mehring, *Karl Marx* (London: Allen and Unwin, 1936); and Heinz F. Peters, *Red Jenny: A Life with Karl Marx* (London: Allen & Unwin, 1986).

CHAPTER 14. Marx in England (pp 145-56)

1. Peters, *Red Jenny*, 100
2. McLellan, *Karl Marx*

BIBLIOGRAPHY

The extracts from the writings of Karl Marx and Frederick Engels used in this book were taken from the following:

Capital: A Critique of Political Economy. Vol. 1, *The Process of Capitalist Production.* Chicago: Charles H. Kerr, 1906. This work was originally published as *Das Kapital: Kritik der politischen Oekonomie,* Vol. 1, *Der Produktionsprozess des Kapitals,* by Otto Meissner in Hamburg in 1867. It was first published in England by Swan Sonnenschein and Co. in 1886, translated from the third German edition (1883) by Samuel Moore and Edward Averling. The first American edition (1906) is the third edition as revised and amplified by Ernest Untermann from the fourth German edition (edited and enlarged by F. Engels and published by Meissner in 1890).

Capital: A Critique of Political Economy. Vol. 2, *The Process of Circulation of Capital.* Chicago: Charles H. Kerr, 1907. A translation by Ernest Untermann of the second German edition (probably 1893) of *Das Kapital: Kritik der politischen Oekonomie,* Vol. 2, *Der Circulationprozess des Kapitals,* originally published by Otto Meissner in Hamburg in 1885.

Capital: A Critique of Political Economy. Vol. 3, *The Process of Capitalist Production as a Whole.* Chicago: Charles H. Kerr, 1909. A translation by Ernest Untermann of the first German edition of *Das Kapital: Kritik der politischen Oekonomie,* Vol. 3, *Der Gesamtprozess der kapitalistischen Produktion,* originally published by Otto Meissner in Hamburg in 1894.

A Contribution to the Critique of Political Economy. Chicago: Charles H. Kerr, 1904. This work was originally published as *Zur Kritik der politischen Oekonomie* by Franz Duncker in Berlin in 1859. The translation, by N.I. Stoke, "with an appendix containing Marx's introduction to the *Critique,* recently published among his posthumous papers," was made from the second German edition, published by J.H.W. Dietz in Stuttgart in 1897.

A Critique of the Gotha Programme. With appendices by Marx, Engels, and Lenin. A revised translation, based on the Russian edition of the Marx, Engels, Lenin Institute. Edited by C.P. Dutton. New York: International Publishers, 1938. This work is based on marginal notes written by Marx in 1875 on a copy of the program of the German Workers' party at Gotha in 1875. These notes, a severe criticism, were sent in a letter to Wilhelm Bracke, and were published by Engels in 1891 in *Die Neue Zeit* under the title *Zur Kritik des sozialdemokratischen Parteiprogramms aus dem Nachlass von Karl Marx.* The first English translation, *The Gotha Program by K. Marx and Did Marx Err?* by Daniel DeLeon, National Executive Committee, Socialist Labor party, was published in New York in 1922.

"Wage Labor and Capital." In *The Essentials of Marx.* By Karl Marx and Frederick Engels. With Introduction and Notes by Algernon Lee. New York: Vanguard Press, 1926. This work, based on lectures given by Marx in 1847 before the German Workingmen's Club in Brussels, originally appeared as columns in the *Neue Rheinische Zeitung* in April 1849. It was published as a pamphlet in Zurich in 1884.

The German Ideology. By Karl Marx and Frederick Engels. Edited with an introduction by R. Pascal. New York: International Publishers, 1939. This work was written in 1845-46 as *Die Deutsche Ideologie: Kritik der neuesten deutschen Philosophie in ihren Repräsentanten Feuerbach, B. Bauer und Steiner, und des deutschen Sozialismus in seinen verschiedenen Propheten.* A small part was apparently published as an article in 1847. Other parts were published in *Dokumente des Sozialismus* by Eduard Bernstein in 1902-3; and still another part was published by G. Mayer in *Archiv für Sozialwissenschaft und Sozialpolitik* in 1921. Parts 1 and 3, translated by W. Looch and C.P. Magill, were published as *The German Ideology* by Lawrence and Wishart in London in 1938.

Manifesto of the Communist Party. By Karl Marx and Frederick Engels. Authorized English translation. Edited and annotated by Frederick Engels. Translated by Samuel Moore. New York: International Publishers, 1932. Three anonymous editions of the *Manifest des Kommunistischen Partei* appeared in 1848, two with J.E. Burghard as printer, and the third with R. Hirschfeld. An English translation, by Helen MacFarlane, was published in the *Red Republican* in London in 1850.

Bibliography

The Poverty of Philosophy. With a preface by Frederick Engels. Translated by H. Quelch. Chicago: Charles H. Kerr, 1920. This was originally published as *Misère de la Philosophie: Response a la Philosophie de la Misère de M. Proudhon* by A. Franck in Paris in 1847.

Theories of Surplus Value. Selections. Translated from the German by G.A. Bonner and Emile Burns. New York: International Publishers, 1952. The original work, edited by Karl Kautsky, was published in three volumes, as *Theorien über den Mehrwert* by J.H.W. Dietz in Stuttgart between 1905 and 1910.

INDEX

ABOUT THE AUTHOR

ROBERT FREEDMAN was born in Boston, Massachusetts, and studied at Boston University, the New School for Social Research, the University of Connecticut, and Yale University, from which he received his Ph.D. in economics.

Professor Freedman has taught at the University of Connecticut and most recently at Colgate University, where he was chairman of the economics department when he retired in 1988.

His publications include *Marx on Economics, Marxist Social Thought*, and articles on a variety of economic subjects.